A NavPress Bible study on the book of

1 CORINTHIANS

NAVPRESS ▲®

A MINISTRY OF THE NAVIGATORS
P.O. BOX 35001, COLORADO SPRINGS, COLORADO 80935

The Navigators is an international Christian organization. Jesus Christ gave His followers the Great Commission to go and make disciples (Matthew 28:19). The aim of The Navigators is to help fulfill that commission by multiplying laborers for Christ in every nation.

NavPress is the publishing ministry of The Navigators. NavPress publications are tools to help Christians grow. Although publications alone cannot make disciples or change lives, they can help believers learn biblical discipleship, and apply what they learn to their lives and ministries.

Fifth printing, 1994

Most Scripture quotations are from the *Holy Bible: New International Version* (NIV). Copyright © 1973, 1978, 1984, International Bible Society. Used by permission of Zondervan Bible Publishers. Other versions used are the *New American Standard Bible* (NASB), © The Lockman Foundation 1960, 1962, 1963, 1968, 1971, 1972, 1973, 1975, 1977; the *Revised Standard Version Bible* (RSV), copyright 1946, 1952, 1971 by the Division of Christian Education of the National Council of the Churches of Christ in the USA, used by permission, all rights reserved; *The New Testament in Modern English* (PH), J.B. Phillips Translator, © J.B. Phillips 1958, 1960, 1972, used by permission of Macmillan Publishing Company; and the *King James Version* (KJV).

Printed in the United States of America

CONTENTS

ACKNOWLEDGMENTS

The LIFECHANGE series has been produced through the coordinated efforts of a team of Navigator Bible study developers and NavPress editorial staff, along with a nationwide network of fieldtesters.

SERIES EDITOR: KAREN HINCKLEY

HOW TO USE THIS STUDY

Objectives

Most guides in the LIFECHANGE series of Bible studies cover one book of the Bible. Although the LIFECHANGE guides vary with the books they explore, they share some common goals:

1. To provide you with a firm foundation of understanding and a thirst to return to the book;

2. To teach you by example how to study a book of the Bible without structured guides;

3. To give you all the historical background, word definitions, and explanatory notes you need, so that your only other reference is the Bible;

4. To help you grasp the message of the book as a whole;

5. To teach you how to let God's Word transform you into Christ's image.

Each lesson in this study is designed to take 60 to 90 minutes to complete on your own. The guide is based on the assumption that you are completing one lesson per week, but if time is limited you can do half a lesson per week or whatever amount allows you to be thorough.

Flexibility

LIFECHANGE guides are flexible, allowing you to adjust the quantity and depth of your study to meet your individual needs. The guide offers many optional questions in addition to the regular numbered questions. The optional questions, which appear in the margins of the study pages, include the following:

Optional Application. Nearly all application questions are optional; we hope you will do as many as you can without overcommitting yourself.

For Thought and Discussion. Beginning Bible students should be able to handle these, but even advanced students need to think about them. These questions frequently deal with ethical issues and other biblical principles. They often offer cross-references to spark thought, but the references do not give obvious answers. They are good for group discussions.

For Further Study. These include: a) cross-references that shed light on a topic the book discusses, and b) questions that delve deeper into the passage. You can omit them to shorten a lesson without missing a major point of the passage.

If you are meeting in a group, decide together which optional questions to prepare for each lesson, and how much of the lesson you will cover at the next meeting. Normally, the group leader should make this decision, but you might let each member choose his or her own application questions.

As you grow in your walk with God, you will find the LIFECHANGE guide growing with you—a helpful reference on a topic, a continuing challenge for application, a source of questions for many levels of growth.

Overview and Details

The study begins with an overview of the book of 1 Corinthians. The key to interpretation is context—what is the whole passage or book *about?*—and the key to context is purpose—what is the author's *aim* for the whole work? In lesson one you will lay the foundation for your study of 1 Corinthians by asking yourself, "Why did the author (and God) write the book? What did they want to accomplish? What is the book about?"

In lessons two through seventeen you will analyze successive passages of 1 Corinthians in detail.

In lesson seventeen you will review 1 Corinthians, returning to the big picture to see whether your view of it has changed after closer study. Review will also strengthen your grasp of major issues and give you an idea of how you have grown from your study.

Kinds of Questions

Bible study on your own—without a structured guide—follows a progression. First you observe: What does the passage *say?* Then you interpret: What does the passage *mean?* Lastly you apply: How does this truth *affect* my life?

Some of the "how" and "why" questions will take some creative thinking, even prayer, to answer. Some are opinion questions without clear-cut right answers; these will lend themselves to discussions and side studies.

Don't let your study become an exercise of knowledge alone. Treat the passage as God's Word, and stay in dialogue with Him as you study. Pray, "Lord, what do You want me to see here?" "Father, why is this true?" "Lord, how does this apply to my life?"

It is important that you write down your answers. The act of writing clarifies your thinking and helps you to remember.

Study Aids

A list of reference materials, including a few notes of explanation to help you make good use of them, begins on page 165. This guide is designed to include enough background to let you interpret with just your Bible and the guide. Still, if you want more information on a subject or want to study a book on your own, try the references listed.

Scripture Versions

Unless otherwise indicated, the Bible quotations in this guide are from the New International Version of the Bible. Other versions cited are the New American Standard Bible (NASB), the Revised Standard Version Bible (RSV), The New Testament in Modern English (PH), and the King James Version (KJV).

Use any translation you like for study, preferably more than one. A paraphrase such as The Living Bible is not accurate enough for study, but it can be helpful for comparison or devotional reading.

Memorizing and Meditating

A psalmist wrote, "I have hidden your word in my heart that I might not sin against you" (Psalm 119:11). If you write down a verse or passage that challenges or encourages you, and reflect on it often for a week or more, you will find it beginning to affect your motives and actions. We forget quickly what we read once; we remember what we ponder.

When you find a significant verse or passage, you might copy it onto a card to keep with you. Set aside five minutes during each day just to think about what the passage might mean in your life. Recite it over to yourself, exploring its meaning. Then, return to your passage as often as you can during your day, for a brief review. You will soon find it coming to mind spontaneously.

For Group Study

A group of four to ten people allows the richest discussions, but you can adapt this guide for other sized groups. It will suit a wide range of group types, such as home Bible studies, growth groups, youth groups, and businessmen's studies. Both new and experienced Bible students, and new and mature Christians, will benefit from the guide. You can omit or leave for later years any questions you find too easy or too hard.

The guide is intended to lead a group through one lesson per week. However, feel free to split lessons if you want to discuss them more thoroughly. Or, omit some questions in a lesson if preparation or discussion time is limited. You can always return to this guide for personal study later. You will be able to discuss only a few questions at length, so choose some for discussion and others for background. Make time at each discussion for members to ask about anything they didn't understand.

Each lesson in the guide ends with a section called "For the group." These sections give advice on how to focus a discussion, how you might apply the lesson in your group, how you might shorten a lesson, and so on. The group leader should read each "For the group" at least a week ahead so that he or she can tell the group how to prepare for the next lesson.

Each member should prepare for a meeting by writing answers for all of the background and discussion questions to be covered. If the group decides not to take an hour per week for private preparation, then expect to take at least two meetings per lesson to work through the questions. Application will be very difficult, however, without private thought and prayer.

Two reasons for studying in a group are accountability and support. When each member commits in front of the rest to seek growth in an area of life, you can pray with one another, listen jointly for God's guidance, help one another to resist temptation, assure each other that the other's growth matters to you, use the group to practice spiritual principles, and so on. Pray about one another's commitments and needs at most meetings. Spend the first few minutes of each meeting sharing any results from applications prompted by previous lessons. Then discuss new applications toward the end of the meeting. Follow such sharing with prayer for these and other needs.

If you write down each other's applications and prayer requests, you are more likely to remember to pray for them during the week, ask about them at the next meeting, and notice answered prayers. You might want to get a notebook for prayer requests and discussion notes.

Notes taken during discussion will help you to remember, follow up on ideas, stay on the subject, and clarify a total view of an issue. But don't let note-taking keep you from participating. Some groups choose one member at each meeting to take notes. Then someone copies the notes and distributes them at the next meeting. Rotating these tasks can help include people. Some groups have someone take notes on a large pad of paper or erasable marker board (preformed shower wallboard works well), so that everyone can see what has been recorded.

Pages 167-168 list some good sources of counsel for leading group studies. The *Small Group Letter*, published by NavPress, is unique, offering insights from experienced leaders every other month.

OVERVIEW

Paul and Corinth

Map for 1 Corinthians

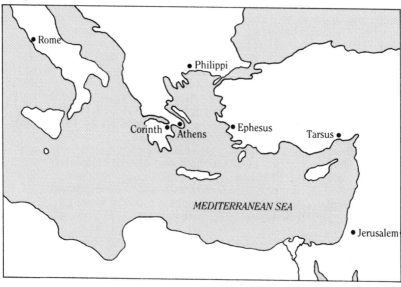

Founding the church in Corinth had been no easy matter for Paul, and maintaining it was proving to be just as challenging. He had planted the faith in the pagan soil of a bustling port city, and weeds persistently threatened to choke it. From Paul's correspondence with the Corinthian believers, we see how he applied the gospel to a host of issues, including sex, intellectualism, public worship, and spiritual gifts.

Saul the Pharisee

Some knowledge of Paul's background helps us understand his views on the issues being debated in Corinth. He was born in the first decade AD in Tarsus, a prosperous city on the trade route from Syria to Asia Minor. Tarsus was known for its schools of philosophy and liberal arts, and some scholars believe that Paul must have had some contact with these. Like most cities in the Roman Empire, Tarsus probably contained synagogues of Greek-speaking Jews who were often as devout as their Hebrew-speaking brethren.[1]

However, Paul called himself "a Hebrew of Hebrews" (Philippians 3:5), which probably means that his parents spoke Hebrew and raised him in a strict Jewish home, isolated as much as possible from the pagan city around them.[2] They named their boy "Saul" after Israel's first king, the most glorious member of the tribe of Benjamin, to which Saul's parents traced their ancestry (Philippians 3:5). It was a rare Jew outside Palestine who could trace a pure lineage back to the ancient days of Israel, and fellow Jews would have envied the pedigree. Furthermore, Saul's family must have owned property and had some importance in the Gentile community as well, for Saul was born not only a citizen of Tarsus (Acts 21:39) but also of Rome (Acts 22:27-28).[3]

Saul's parents had such aspirations that they sent their son to study Jewish law in Jerusalem under the foremost rabbi of the day, the Pharisee Gamaliel (Acts 22:3, Galatians 1:14). With Gamaliel, Saul learned a little about Greek rhetoric and oratory, and a lot about Jewish reasoning, arguing, and the Law. The Pharisees (the Hebrew word means "the separated ones") felt that God had set them apart to live by the *Torah* (the Law or Teaching of Moses). For them, this meant following the interpretations of the Torah laid down by generations of teachers. Some Pharisees held that a man was righteous if he had done more good than bad, but Saul apparently followed the stricter group who insisted that even the least implications of the Law must be kept.[4]

The Pharisees expected a *Messiah* (Hebrew for "Anointed One"; Greek meaning "Christ") who would deliver them from oppression and rule with justice. However, Jesus of Nazareth had infuriated many Pharisees by interpreting the Torah differently and claiming a special relationship with God. Thus, when some Jews began to proclaim Jesus as Messiah and Lord (Lord was a term usually reserved for God), strict Pharisees opposed them vehemently.

Saul helped lead the fight against the proclaimers of Jesus Christ in Jerusalem (Acts 7:58-8:3, Galatians 1:13). When some followers of Christ were driven out, Saul obtained permission to pursue them to Damascus. But on the way there, Jesus confronted Saul in a blinding encounter (Acts 9:1-19), revealing to Saul that he was persecuting the very God he professed to worship. From then on, Saul's understanding of God and Torah began to change dramatically. He joined those Jews who were urging other Jews to believe in Jesus, and after some years God called him to proclaim Jesus as Savior to the Gentiles also. Saul took the Greek name "Paul" when he turned to work among Gentiles.

Timeline of Paul's Ministry

(All dates are approximate, based on F.F. Bruce, *Paul: Apostle of the Heart Set Free*, page 475.)

Public ministry of Jesus	28-30 AD
Conversion of Paul (Acts 9:1-19)	33
Paul visits Jerusalem to see Peter (Galatians 1:18)	35
Paul in Cilicia and Syria (Acts 9:30, Galatians 1:21)	35-46
Paul visits Jerusalem to clarify the mission to the Gentiles (Galatians 2:1-10)	46
Paul and Barnabas in Cyprus and Galatia (Acts 13-14)	47-48
Letter to the Galatians	48?
Council of Jerusalem (Acts 15)	49
Paul and Silas travel from Antioch to Asia Minor, Macedonia, and Achaia (Acts 16-17)	49-50
Letters to the Thessalonians	50
Paul in Corinth (Acts 18:1-18)	50-52
Paul visits Jerusalem	52
Paul in Ephesus (Acts 19)	52-55
Letters to the Corinthians	55-56
Paul travels to Macedonia, Dalmatia, and Achaia (Acts 20)	55-57
Letter to the Romans	early 57
Paul to Jerusalem (Acts 21:1-23:22)	May 57
Paul imprisoned in Caesarea (Acts 23:23-26:32)	57-59
Paul sent to house arrest in Rome (Acts 27:1-28:31)	59-62
Letters to Philippians, Colossians, Ephesians, and Philemon	60?-62
Letters to Timothy and Titus	?
Paul executed in Rome	65?

11

Paul the missionary

Paul spent ten years in the Roman provinces of Cilicia and Syria (Galatians 1:21), probably preaching Jesus along with Greek-speaking Jewish Christians. Then a believer named Barnabas called him to Syrian Antioch, where by this time rapid conversions had made the church more Gentile than Jewish.[5] After a while, the church in Antioch commissioned Paul and Barnabas to evangelize the provinces of Cyprus and Galatia. The two men succeeded in founding churches in several cities. Indeed, the mission to the Gentiles was so successful that the apostles in Jerusalem invited Paul and Barnabas to a council to clarify exactly what God expected of Gentile believers (Acts 15). Paul spent the eight years after the council in Jerusalem planting more churches. He went first to Macedonia, where he founded churches in Philippi, Thessalonica, and Berea (Acts 16:1-17:15). Trouble from the Jews in Macedonia drove him south to Greece. He received a cold reception in Athens, so he traveled on to Corinth, the capital of the Roman province of Achaia (modern Greece).

Paul and his mission team spent a year and a half in Corinth to found a church firmly in that important city (Acts 18:1-18). When things looked solid in Corinth, Paul sailed back east to Antioch and Jerusalem, then traveled west again to plant a church in Ephesus, the capital of the province of Asia (part of modern Turkey). Meanwhile, the church at Corinth received a great blessing in the person of another stellar Christian leader. A former Jew named Apollos arrived to teach the faith and debate Corinthian Jews who opposed Christianity (Acts 18:24-28).

Toward the end of his three-year stay in Ephesus, Paul began to receive disturbing news from Corinth. He wrote a letter (now lost) instructing the Corinthian believers not to associate with church members who practiced illicit sex (1 Corinthians 5:9). Sometime later, members of the household of a believer named Chloe brought news that the Corinthian church was splitting into factions, each of which claimed some prominent leader as its authority (1 Corinthians 1:11). Then three members of the church brought Paul a letter from the whole body (1 Corinthians 7:1, 16:17). This letter was full of questions about various issues, but the messengers also reported scandalous information: incest, class snobbery, and other problems were infecting the church. In response to these ills, Paul dictated a long letter—the one we call 1 Corinthians.

Corinth

Paul spent more time in Corinth and Ephesus than in any other cities he visited (besides Rome and Caesarea, where he was imprisoned), for as two of the most important trading centers in the Empire, they were promising hubs for evangelism. A strong church in Corinth could spread the gospel not only throughout Greece, but through trading connections all over the known world. Likewise, a fractured or heretical church in Corinth could either collapse or spread a false gospel throughout the world.

The Romans utterly demolished Corinth in 146 BC for resisting Roman domination, but Julius Caesar rebuilt it a century later as a Roman colony. As a colony, it was populated primarily with Roman citizens, but as a commercial center, it was soon full also of Greeks, Syrians, Asians, Egyptians, and a large community of Jews. It is estimated that in Paul's day 250,000 free persons and some 400,000 slaves inhabited Corinth, not to mention the thousands of tradesmen, sailors, and tourists who visited.[6] Because of its cosmopolitan flavor, Corinth was considered the least Greek of the Greek cities and the least Roman of the Roman colonies.[7]

The source of Corinth's prosperity was commerce. The city sat astride the narrow isthmus that connected mainland Greece with the peninsula called the Peloponnese. Because weather and rocks made it hazardous to sail around the Peloponnese, it was far less costly for ships to go through Corinth. They would dock at the harbor of Cenchrea (east of Corinth on the Saronic Gulf). There, large ships would unload their cargo onto wagons, which would haul the cargo on a sort of wooden railway (the *diolkos*) to the harbor of Lechaeum (west of Corinth on the Corinthian Gulf). Smaller ships were hauled fully loaded across the three and a half miles of the *diolkos*. Thus, the most sensible way to get anything to Rome from Ephesus, China, or Egypt was through Corinth.

Corinth's prosperity led to luxury and licentiousness. Indeed, in polite Greek, the word "to Corinthianize" meant "to practice sexual immorality" or "to debauch." The most notorious of Corinth's dozen temples was dedicated to Aphrodite, the goddess of love. About a thousand female slaves staffed the temple to practice ritual prostitution with worshipers (including sailors and tourists). This was a profitable attraction and contributed both to Corinth's prosperity and her reputation.[8] Yet Corinth also had prestige. In Greek jargon, a person who spoke "Corinthian words" had pretentions to philosophy and learning. The Isthmian Games, which were second in importance only to the Olympic Games, were celebrated every other year under Corinth's governance.[9] And Corinth was both the capital of Achaia and its richest city. In short, wealth, loose morals, and intellectual pride were the Corinthian hallmarks.

First Corinthians

Predictably, wealth, loose morals, and intellectual pride lay at the root of the troubles in the Corinthian church. There were divisions between those members who liked Paul's simple style and those who preferred a more sophisticated and philosophical approach to religion. There was strife between those who thought freedom in Christ meant liberation from "outworn" taboos about sex and food, those who felt that Jewish and other rules must be kept strictly, and those who believed something in between. There was jealousy between those who possessed the kind of flashy spiritual gifts that suggested true enlightenment and those who did not. And there was bitterness between the rich and the poor. All this Paul addressed in his letter, at the same time dispatching his aide Timothy to help sort things out in person. First Corinthians is not a doctrinal treatise but a pastor's response to problems, yet it is the source of some of our most helpful information about Christian faith and practice.

First impressions

It is much easier to study a book passage by passage if you have first examined it as a whole. An overview is especially necessary if you have never studied the book before. Below are some suggestions for an overview of 1 Corinthians. Look over questions 1 through 5 before you begin.

Study Skill—Interpreting Epistles
The hardest thing about understanding biblical letters is that we have only half of the correspondence. That is, we know what Paul said, but we don't know anything else about the situations he was responding to, the people he was writing to, or the questions they were asking. It is a little like listening to one end of a telephone conversation and trying to figure out what is being said on the other end. Often—with matters ranging from the Cephas party (who were they, and what did they believe?) in 1:12 to "baptized for the dead" (what on earth is this?) in 15:29—we can only guess. In order to make educated guesses rather than wild speculations, we need to be careful detectives observing every clue.

As you read 1 Corinthians for the first time, don't try to answer every question about what is going on. Don't try to absorb every detail. Look for the main ideas, the threads that tie paragraphs together, and the questions you want to answer for yourself later. This broad overview is essential preparation for the close detective work later on.

---

1. What if you could have been one of the Corinthian Christians who just received this letter from Paul? Read it through once for the overall message, just as you might read any letter. Don't stop to unravel difficult pieces; just try to follow the big ideas.

    As you read, keep a list of repeated words, phrases, and ideas that seem important to Paul's message. (For example, you'll notice that words like *proud, arrogant,* and *puffed up* appear often.) This list will help you notice the main issues Paul is addressing and the main ideas he wants to get across. It will also suggest questions you will want to answer when you study further. (For instance, *spiritual* turns up a lot. What does Paul mean by this term?)

---

2. Jot here any questions that came up during your first reading—any terms or passages you'd like clarified, for example. You can also write down any questions prompted by the introduction on pages 9-14.

_____

_____

_____

_____

_____

Study Skill—Broad Outline
It is often easier to see the big picture of a long book like 1 Corinthians if you make a broad outline during your overview. The best way to do this on your own is to make up a title for each chapter, then try to group the chapters together. As you go along, you'll find that the chapter divisions are not always the best places to break, but they are a place to start. (The chapters of the New Testament were devised several centuries after the books were written. They aid us in finding passages, but they are not inspired by God in the way that the books themselves are.)

3. Below, we've suggested some ways in which you might group the sections of 1 Corinthians. Go back through the book and write down titles that you think express what each smaller section is about. Then write titles for each of the larger sections. (You can change any of the divisions if you like.)

1:1-9 _____

1:10-4:21 _____

   1:10-17 _____

   1:18-3:4 _____

15

3:5-4:5 _____

4:6-21 _____

5:1-6:20 _____

5:1-13 _____

6:1-11 _____

6:12-20 _____

7:1-40 _____

8:1-11:1 _____

8:1-13 _____

9:1-27 _____

10:1-13 _____

10:14-22 _____

10:23-11:1 _____

11:2-14:40 _____

11:2-16 _____

11:17-34 _____

12:1-14:40 _____

15:1-58 _____

16:1-24 _____

4. What do you observe about Paul as a person from his letter to the Corinthians? (Is he proud, humble, intelligent, slow of mind, passionate, cool . . . ?)

_____

_____

_____

_____

_____

5. How would you summarize what this letter as a whole is about? What are its main themes? What is Paul's overall purpose for writing it?

_____

_____

_____

_____

_____

Study Skill—Application

When we observe and interpret what a biblical book says and means, we often have to think about its human author and first-century readers. It is important to understand what God was saying to them in their situation before we decide what He is saying to us in ours. Nevertheless, 2 Timothy 3:16-17 tells us that "All Scripture is God-breathed and is useful for teaching, rebuking, correcting and training in righteousness, so that the man of God may be thoroughly equipped for every good work." James 1:22 urges us to do what the Word says, not merely hear it. Therefore, the last step of Bible study should always be to ask yourself, "What difference should this passage make to my life? How should it make me want to think or act?" Application will require time, thought, prayer, and perhaps even discussion with another person.

At times you may find it most productive to concentrate on one specific application, giving it careful thought and prayer. At other times you may want to list many implications a passage of Scripture has for your life, meditating on them all for several days before you choose one for concentrated prayer and action. Use whatever method helps you take to heart and act on what the passage says.

6. How is the overall message of 1 Corinthians relevant to your life? What actions or matters for prayer and thought does your first reading of this book encourage you to pursue?

_____

_____

_____

_____

_____

17

For the group

This "For the group" section and the ones in later lessons are intended to suggest ways of structuring your discussions. Feel free to select what suits your group and ignore the rest. The main goals of this lesson are to get to know 1 Corinthians as a whole and the people with whom you are going to study it.

Worship. Some groups like to begin with prayer and/or singing. Some share requests for prayer at the beginning, but leave the actual prayer until after the study. Others prefer just to chat and have refreshments for a while and then move to the study, leaving worship until the end. It is a good idea to start with at least a brief prayer for the Holy Spirit's guidance and some silence to help everyone change focus from the day's busyness to the Scripture.

Warm-up. The beginning of a new study is a good time to lay a foundation for honest sharing of ideas, to get comfortable with each other, and to encourage a sense of common purpose. One way to establish common ground is to talk about what each group member hopes to get out of your group—out of your study of 1 Corinthians, and out of any prayer, singing, sharing, outreach, or anything else you might do together. Why do you want to study the Bible, and 1 Corinthians in particular? If you have someone write down each member's hopes and expectations, then you can look back at these goals later to see if they are being met. Allow about fifteen minutes for this discussion so that it does not degenerate into vague chatting.

How to use this study. If the group has never used a LIFECHANGE study guide before, you might take a whole meeting to get acquainted, discuss your goals, and go over the "How to Use This Study" section on pages 5-8. Then you can take a second meeting to discuss the overview. This will assure that everyone understands the study and will give you more time to read all of 1 Corinthians and answer the overview questions.

Go over the parts of the "How to Use This Study" section that you think the group should especially notice. For example, point out the optional questions in the margins. These are available as group discussion questions, ideas for application, and suggestions for further study. It is unlikely that anyone will have time or desire to answer all the optional questions. A person might do one "Optional Application" for any given lesson. You might choose one or two "For Thought and Discussion" questions for your group discussion, or you might spend all your time on the numbered questions. If someone wants to write answers to the optional questions, suggest that he use a separate notebook. It will also be helpful for discussion notes, prayer requests, answers to prayers, application plans, and so on.

Invite everyone to ask questions about how to use the study guide and how your discussions will go.

Reading. It is often helpful to refresh everyone's memory by reading the passage aloud before discussing the questions. Reading all of 1 Corinthians is probably out of the question, but you might ask someone to read 1:1-17, using the tone of voice he or she thinks Paul would have used in speaking these words. Try to make the chapter sound like a living person talking to a real group of people he knows.

Introduction. Ask a few questions about the background material, such as, "What do you think are the important things we should know about Paul? About the city of Corinth? About the church in Corinth?" Group members don't need to memorize all of the information on pages 9-14, but that material should help them understand the people and situations that lie behind 1 Corinthians. The more real the people and circumstances are to you, the easier it will be for you to interpret the letter.

First impressions. Give everyone a chance to answer questions 1, 2, 4, and 5. Make a master list of all the repeated words, phrases, and ideas that everyone observed. Make another list of everyone's questions. You probably won't want to answer those questions now, but you should keep them handy and return to them at appropriate points in your study.

Next, compare your outlines (question 3). You might also want to compare them to outlines you find in study Bibles or commentaries. If you do, observe both what all the outlines have in common and how they differ. Which approaches do you find most helpful?

Let everyone respond to question 6. If some group members are unfamiliar with applying Scripture to their lives, plan to take time at your next meeting to discuss how to do this and to brainstorm some possible applications. The Study Skill in lesson two may be of help.

Wrap-up. The group leader should have read lesson two and its "For the group" section. At this point, he or she might give a short summary of what members can expect in that lesson and the coming meeting. This is a chance to whet everyone's appetite, assign any optional questions, omit any numbered questions, or forewarn members of possible difficulties.

Encourage any members who found the overview especially difficult. Some people are better at seeing the big picture than others. Some are best at analyzing a particular verse or paragraph, while others are strongest at seeing how a passage applies to their lives. Urge members to give thanks for their own and others' strengths, and to give and request help when needed. The group is a place to learn from each other. Later lessons will draw on the gifts of close analyzers as well as overviewers and appliers, practical as well as theoretical thinkers.

Worship. Many groups like to end with singing and/or prayer. This can include songs and prayers that respond to what you've learned in 1 Corinthians or prayers for specific needs of group members.

Some people are shy about sharing personal needs or praying aloud in groups, especially before they know the other people well. If this is true of your group, then a song and/or some silent prayer and a short closing prayer spoken by the leader might be an appropriate end. You could also share requests and pray in pairs.

1. A. T. Robertson, "Paul, the Apostle," *The International Standard Bible Encyclopaedia*, volume 4 (Grand Rapids, Michigan: William B. Eerdmans Publishing Company, 1956), page 2276.
2. F. F. Bruce, *Paul: Apostle of the Heart Set Free* (Grand Rapids, Michigan: William B. Eerdmans Publishing Company, 1977), pages 41-43.
3. Bruce, *Paul*, pages 32-40.
4. Bruce, *Paul*, pages 50-52.
5. Bruce, *Paul*, pages 127-133.
6. *The NIV Study Bible*, edited by Kenneth Barker (Grand Rapids, Michigan: Zondervan Corporation, 1985), page 1732.
7. Leon Morris, *The First Epistle of Paul to the Corinthians* (Grand Rapids, Michigan: William B. Eerdmans Publishing Company, 1958), page 16.
8. F. F. Bruce, *1 and 2 Corinthians* (Grand Rapids, Michigan: William B. Eerdmans Publishing Company, 1971), pages 18-19.
9. Morris, page 16; Bruce, *1 and 2 Corinthians*, page 89.

1 CORINTHIANS 1:1-9

To the Called

The news from Chloe's people and the letter brought by Stephanas and the rest have spurred Paul to dictate an urgent letter. But he is not abrupt; as is customary in Greek letters, he begins by politely identifying himself and the letter's recipients, and he continues with a few kind words before the meat of the message. Yet Paul never wastes words. Features that are mere polite nothings in the average Greek letter are all given Christian flavor and made to introduce the themes of the epistle.

Read 1:1-9 carefully, preferably in more than one translation. (A second version can illuminate different facets by using different words.) Watch for words and ideas Paul repeats and for themes that are echoed later in the letter. Ask God to open your mind and heart to observe and understand.

Greeting (1:1-3)

Apostle (1:1). Literally, "one who is sent"—a messenger, proxy, ambassador. In Jewish law, the *apostolos* (Greek) or *shaliach* (Aramaic) was a person acting with full authority for another in a business or legal transaction.[1]

The New Testament apostle is not just a delivery service, but an authoritative messenger of God (John 20:21). The Church recognized certain men who had seen the risen Jesus as apostles, the leaders with the highest authority regarding doctrine and policy.

Sosthenes (1:1). Possibly the ruler of the Corinthian synagogue (Acts 18:17). If so, he became a Christian either during or after Paul's ministry there, and he was at Ephesus with Paul when this letter was written. However, the name is not uncommon, so it may be a different man.

Holy (1:2). "Saints" in NASB, meaning "set apart ones." Likewise, ***sanctified*** means "set apart for God" or "made holy." Paul stresses his readers' identity as holy ones twice in this verse.

Grace (1:3). The normal Greek greeting was *chai-rein*, meaning "greetings" or "favor from me to you." Paul preferred a related word, *charis*, which means God's favor bestowed on people. Grace includes both the gift of salvation and God's daily empowering presence, which He bestows on His people to be and do what He has called them to be and do.

Peace (1:3). This was the common Jewish greeting. It meant wholeness and well-being in all aspects of life—health, harmony between people, a flourishing earth, and so on. To wish someone peace was to wish him or her a foretaste of the Messianic Age foretold by the prophets, a taste of God's presence and the fulfillment that flows from that presence.[2]

1. Paul chooses his words carefully in identifying himself and his readers. In light of the topics he will discuss later on, why do you think he . . .

   describes himself as "called to be an apostle of Christ Jesus by the will of God" (1:1)? (Consider 1:10-12, 3:4-5, 4:1-6, 9:1-6, 11:1.)

   _____

   _____

   _____

   _____

names his readers "those sanctified in Christ Jesus and called to be holy" (1:2)? (See, for example, 3:1-4; 5:1-2,6-8; 6:9-20.)

_____

_____

_____

_____

_____

Thanksgiving (1:4-9)

_____

Blameless (1:8). Not faultless in the sense of never having erred, but "unimpeachable"—no one will be able to bring a charge against those whom God has chosen (Romans 8:33).[3]

The day of our Lord Jesus Christ (1:8). In the writings of the Old Testament prophets, "the day of the LORD" was the day when God would intervene in history to show Himself Lord of the earth, bringing justice to the righteous and the wicked (Isaiah 2:11,17,20; Joel 2:1-11,28-32; Amos 5:18-20). In the New Testament, that day is the one on which Christ will be **revealed** (1 Corinthians 1:7) as Lord of all at His second coming, and on which He will bring justice to the earth.

It is Paul's continual habit to take Old Testament scriptures and ideas that referred to "the LORD" (God) and apply them to Jesus Christ (1 Corinthians 2:16 is another example of this).

Fellowship (1:9). The Greek word _koinonia_ means communion, participation, partnership, fellowship. It denotes relationship and joint activity in a family or an enterprise. Fellowship with Jesus Christ is such an intimate, personal thing that Paul frequently speaks of believers as being "in" Christ (1:2,30)—united with this Person and so dependent upon and surrounded by Him that He is the very atmosphere we breathe.

For Thought and Discussion: What phrase does Paul repeat with slight variations nine times in 1:1-9? What does this persistent reiteration tell you about Paul's emphasis?

For Thought and Discussion: Why does Paul need to emphasize to the Corinthians that Christ will be revealed on the coming day of the Lord (1:6-8)? Think about 15:12-34.

23

For Thought and Discussion: How is the "testimony about Christ . . . confirmed" in a person (1:6)? That is, how does a person become living confirmation that the gospel is true?

For Thought and Discussion: Does Paul mean that each Corinthian has every gift, or that the church as a whole lacks no gift (1:7)? Why do you think so?

2. It was Paul's custom to begin his letters by thanking God for the best traits of his readers. For what traits of the Corinthians does Paul thank God (1:4-9)?

_____

_____

_____

_____

_____

3. How is this thanksgiving relevant to the rest of the letter? (Consider 4:7; 12:1,4-26.)

_____

_____

_____

_____

_____

4. Circle the statements below that are true of you.

"In him [Christ] you have been enriched in every way" (1:5).

"Our testimony about Christ was confirmed in you" (1:6).

"You do not lack any spiritual gift as you eagerly wait for our Lord Jesus" (1:7).

"He will keep you strong to the end, so that you will be blameless" (1:8).

5. What is one difference that these truths should make to your attitudes and actions?

_____

_____

_____

_____

Study Skill—Observation
The simplest way to make detailed observa-
tions is sometimes just to make lists under
various topics. You can even keep a running
list throughout your study of a book. Some
possible topics might be, "Truths about God,"
"Truths about Christ," "Truths about the Holy
Spirit," "Truths about Our Identity in Christ,"
"Attitudes I Should Have," "Ways I Should
Act," "Priorities I Should Have."

**Optional
Application:** a. What
are the implications
for your life of the fact
that God is faithful
about keeping you
strong until the end
(1:8-9)?
b. In what other
ways is God faithful to
you? How should this
affect your actions?

6. Make a list of all the truths about God that Paul
   affirms in 1:1-9.

_____

_____

_____

_____

_____

_____

_____

7. Choose one of these truths and explain why it is
   personally important to you.

_____

_____

_____

_____

Study Skill—Application
It can be helpful to plan an application in
several steps:
1. Record the verse or passage that contains the truth you want to apply to your life.
If the passage is short enough, consider copy-
ing it word for word, as an aid to memory.

(continued on page 26)

25

(continued from page 25)

(Memorizing the passage is always a good idea, since you can then meditate on it anytime during the day.)

2. State the truth of the passage that impresses you. For instance, *"Christ will keep me strong to the end, so that I will be blameless on the day of the Lord (1:8)."*

3. Describe how you already see this truth at work positively in your life. (This is a chance to rejoice in what God is doing.) For example, *"With God's strengthening power, I've been able to resist the temptation to sweep my faith under the rug when I'm afraid people will think I'm weird and foolish."*

4. Tell how you fall short in relation to this truth, or how you want the truth to affect your life. (Ask God to enable you to see yourself clearly.) For example, *"I still have a tendency to get wrapped up in acquiring possessions and succeeding materially. I'm still tempted to make my material goals more of a priority than loving, listening to, and obeying Christ. When I find myself slipping from obedience, I often panic and forget that Christ is the One who will keep me strong, if I trust Him. I try to keep myself strong by sheer willpower."*

5. State precisely what you plan to do about having your life changed in this area. (Ask God what, if anything, you can do. Don't forget that transformation depends on His will, power, and timing, not on yours. Diligent prayer should always be part of your application.) For instance, *"I'm going to meditate on 1 Corinthians 1:8 daily this week, and memorize the verse. When I find myself tempted to fall short of what God expects of me, I'm going to remind myself of this verse. Instead of beating up on myself for my failures, I'm going to confess my sins to the Lord each day and thank Him that I can trust Him to keep me strong."*

6. Plan a way to remind yourself to do what you've decided, such as putting a note on your refrigerator or in your office, or asking a friend to remind you.[4]

Your response

8. What truth from 1:1-9 would you like to take to heart this week?

_____

_____

_____

_____

_____

_____

9. How do you already see this truth affecting your life?

_____

_____

_____

_____

_____

10. How do you fall short or want to grow in this area?

_____

_____

_____

_____

_____

_____

11. What can you do to cooperate with God in letting this growth happen?

_____

_____

_____

_____

_____

_____

12. How can you make sure you will do what you have planned?

_____

_____

_____

_____

13. If you have any questions about 1:1-9 or the material in this lesson, record them here.

_____

_____

_____

_____

For the group

Worship.

Warm-up. It often takes time for a group to shift mental gears from the day's business to Bible study. A period of worship can help this transition, and so can a short question that connects the day's experience to the topic at hand. Such a warm-up question can also help you get to know each other better, so that group members will grow more comfortable sharing personal things such as applications. A possible warm-up for this lesson might be, "How have you experienced God's grace this week?"

Read aloud. Ask someone to read 1:1-9 aloud with meaning. Greek sentences are often long and complex, but they are easier to understand if read with pauses at logical places.

Summarize. Take a quick glance at the forest before scrutinizing the trees. Ask someone to tell briefly what Paul says in 1:1-9.

Questions. This lesson emphasizes the connections between Paul's introductory words and the rest of the letter. Other themes are what he says about God and the Corinthians, and how these are relevant to you. You may not be able to cover all of the issues in a passage at equal depth; if not, choose those that you think are most significant for your group. There is nothing wrong with not getting to all the questions if you are digging deeply into the Scriptures.

Many groups like to allow about half of their discussion time to plan applications. This is possible if all of the participants have prepared the lesson ahead of time and understand the passage fairly well. You may find that you need more time just to discuss what a complicated passage means. However, do try to save at least ten minutes for everyone to share what he or she would like to do about what you have studied. If the idea of such purposeful application is new to your group, you might plan extra time to go over the Study Skill on pages 25-26. Some group members may find this systematic approach helpful, while others may find it too structured for their temperaments. Try to help everyone find an approach to application that is effective and suits him or her.

At times you may want to discuss some of the word definitions. Use your judgment to determine which ones might require questions, such as, "What does Paul mean by 'blameless'? How is this different from what we might suppose he means?" It isn't necessary for everyone to absorb all of the material in the definitions; they are there simply to help you interpret the passage.

Summarize and wrap-up. Ask someone to summarize your discussion briefly. What is 1:1-9 about? How, in general, have group members said they want to apply it?

Prayer. Take time to pray for each other, asking God to work in your lives to accomplish the growth each of you has desired. Ask Him to continue to enrich each person in every way. Pray for any specific things that come up.

A good way to close a meeting is to use the passage at hand as a springboard to praise and thanksgiving. For example, thank God for calling you to be holy along with all those everywhere who call on the name of our Lord Jesus Christ. Thank Him for His grace and peace, for all the ways He has enriched you. Thank Him for confirming through your lives and experiences that the testimony about Christ is true. Thank Him for His promise that He will keep you strong to the end, so that you will be blameless on the day when the Lord Jesus Christ is revealed. Thank Him for calling you into fellowship with His Son. Praise Him for His faithfulness to His calls and promises.

1. Erich von Eicken and Helgo Lindner, "Apostle," *The New International Dictionary of New Testament Theology*, volume 1, edited by Colin Brown (Grand Rapids, Michigan: Zondervan Corporation, 1975), pages 126-129.
2. Hartmut Beck and Colin Brown, "Peace," *The New International Dictionary of New Testament Theology*, volume 2, pages 776-783.
3. Morris, page 37.
4. Adapted from "The Five-Point Application" in *The 2:7 Series, Course 3* (Colorado Springs, Colorado: NavPress, 1988), pages 62-63.

1 CORINTHIANS 1:10-2:5

Foolishness

God (says Paul) has called you to be in fellowship with His Son Jesus Christ (1:9). This is no idle cliche. It has direct relevance to what is going on in the Corinthian church. Are the Corinthians living out the implications of fellowship with Jesus? Read 1:10-2:5, trying to follow Paul's train of thought.

Divisions (1:10-17)

Study Skill—Think Paragraphs

In order to grasp what the Holy Spirit is saying to us in a passage of Scripture, it is crucial to grasp the message of the whole passage, not just individual verses. In a letter, the author is usually following a train of thought. A paragraph is the basic unit of thought, and modern translations often mark them to help you follow the thought. So, when you read a passage, *think paragraphs.* Decide for yourself where a unit of thought starts and ends. Ask yourself two questions about each paragraph:

1. What is the author saying here?
2. Why is he saying it here? What does it have to do with what comes before and after?

For instance, 1:10-17 is a unit (the NIV makes it two paragraphs for easier reading;

(continued on page 32)

(continued from page 31)
the NASB makes it one paragraph). In studying 1:10-17, you should first ask yourself what Paul is saying in this paragraph. Then observe what this has to do with what he said in 1:4-9 and what he will say in 1:18-25 and later paragraphs. If you do this, you will notice that 1:10-17 contrasts with the idea of fellowship mentioned in 1:9, that 1:17 introduces the idea of wisdom developed in 1:18-25, and that 1:10-17 introduces the topic Paul discusses at length all the way through 4:21.

Chloe's household (1:11). Chloe is evidently a woman of sufficient means to be running a household with servants, clients, and perhaps children. (It was not uncommon for widows to run their households.) It may be that Chloe's house is in Corinth, and that some of her servants or grown children have come to Ephesus with news. Alternatively, her household may be in Ephesus, and members of it have returned from a visit to Corinth with news.

Apollos (1:12). Acts 18:24-28 tells us that Apollos was a Jew from the city of Alexandria in Egypt. He was "learned," which means that he had been thoroughly trained by the rabbis in the Scriptures. It was fashionable among Alexandrian Jews to interpret the Scriptures symbolically (as allegory) rather than literally. Apollos was probably steeped in this method, and probably also in rhetoric, the intellectual style of oratory and debate that was popular at the time. Thus the style, though not the content, of Apollos's preaching probably differed from Paul's. Apollos went to Corinth to teach and debate the Jews after Paul left there for Ephesus.

Cephas (1:12). The Aramaic form of the name "Peter." We don't know whether Peter went to Corinth at some point and attracted a following among the believers there, or whether certain members of the church were simply using his name as a flag for their faction. Some commentators feel that Peter may have been popular among those Corinthians who liked a more Jewish approach to Christianity than Paul's.

Baptized into the name of (1:13). The name in ancient times stood for the person's whole self. To be baptized *into* someone is to be incorporated into him (12:13)—to enter into fellowship, allegiance, and union with him.

It was apparently Paul's practice to let his colleagues baptize converts rather than doing it himself.

Words of human wisdom (1:17). In the Greek system of education, a gentleman normally studied one of two fields at the university level: philosophy or rhetoric. To speak and reason intellectually were considered the most important skills of a cultured person. Paul sets himself in deliberate contrast with the kind of men who impressed the Corinthians, those who specialized in rhetorical words and human wisdom. (The Greek word *sophia* gives us "philosophy," the love of wisdom.)

For Thought and Discussion: In 1:13-17, is Paul saying that baptism is unimportant? If so, why? If not, what is he saying, and why?

1. Verses 10-17 introduce the topic Paul discusses from 1:10 to 4:21. Describe the problem in the Corinthian church that has been reported to Paul.

_____

_____

_____

_____

_____

Power and wisdom (1:18-31)

2. Basically, what does Paul say in 1:18-31?

_____

_____

For Thought and Discussion: Why is the crucified Messiah "a stumbling block to Jews" (1:23)? (See, for example, Deuteronomy 21:23, Isaiah 9:6-7, Galatians 3:13.) What do the Jews believe about the Messiah that is incompatible with the idea of crucifixion?

_____

_____

_____

3. Paul contrasts "the message of the cross" with "the wisdom of the world." What is "the message of the cross" (1:18)? (*Optional:* See Isaiah 53:4-6, 1 Corinthians 15:3, Philippians 2:6-11, Colossians 1:19-23.)

_____

_____

_____

_____

_____

_____

_____

4. Why is this message . . .

"foolishness to those who are perishing" (1:18)?

_____

_____

_____

_____

"the power of God" to believers (1:18)?

_____

_____

_____

_____

5. According to 1:19-31, why did God choose to express His power through foolishness, weakness, and lowliness?

_____

_____

_____

_____

6. How has "God made foolish the wisdom of the world" (1:20)?

_____

_____

_____

_____

7. What implications do the following statements have for your life?

"For the foolishness of God is wiser than man's wisdom, and the weakness of God is stronger than man's strength" (1:25).

_____

_____

_____

_____

"Let him who boasts boast in the Lord" (1:31).

_____

_____

_____

_____

For Thought and Discussion: Are the unbelievers you know more like the Jews who wanted miraculous signs (practical evidence) to prove the gospel, or more like the Greeks who wanted philosophical proofs? How can you get through to such people with the truth of the gospel?

For Thought and Discussion: a. What is wrong with preaching the gospel with words of human wisdom (1:17)? Why does this empty the Cross of its power?

b. How do you think a modern preacher should apply this verse?

For Further Study: In 1:30, Paul explains that Christ is real wisdom for us in that He is our righteousness, holiness, and redemption. Using a concordance and perhaps a Bible dictionary, find out what righteousness, holiness, and redemption are and how Christ is each of these for us.

For Thought and Discussion: a. Why did Paul think it was good that he came to Corinth in weakness and fear (2:3,5)?
b. Does this encourage you as you take part in spreading the gospel? Why or why not?

8. What does 1:18-31 tell you about God's character, personality, and values?

_____

_____

_____

_____

Paul's methods (2:1-5)

9. How has all this about the world's wisdom and God's wisdom affected the way Paul has conducted himself as a missionary (1:17, 2:1-5)?

_____

_____

_____

_____

10. What does it mean to preach not with eloquence but with a demonstration of the Spirit's power (2:4)? (How is the Spirit's power demonstrated? For answers from the apostles' ministries, you might consider the book of Acts. Also, think about your own experience.)

_____

_____

_____

_____

11. How is 1:18–2:5 relevant to the problem of factions in Corinth?

_____

_____

_____

_____

36

Your response

12. What one insight from 1:10-2:5 would you like to take to heart?

_____

_____

_____

_____

_____

13. How have you seen this truth already active in your life?

_____

_____

_____

_____

_____

14. How would you like this truth to affect you in deeper ways?

_____

_____

_____

_____

_____

15. What steps can you take to cooperate with God in bringing this about?

_____

_____

_____

_____

_____

16. List any questions you have about 1:10-2:5.

_____

_____

_____

_____

For the group

Warm-up. Here are two possibilities:
1. How would you describe your worldly status? In the world, would people consider you to be wise, intellectual, influential, or from a prestigious family?
2. What convinced you to believe the gospel? For instance, was it factual evidence, intellectual reasoning, emotional attraction, the lives of people you knew?

Read aloud and summarize. 1:10-2:5 is a long passage. You may want to have different people read sections.

Questions. You may need to skip lightly over some of the questions in order to allow time to discuss applications. When you get to application, ask if anyone has any questions or learned anything about application after doing it for the past week. Don't expect vast results from such a short time; just share anything you've learned.

Summarize and wrap-up.

Prayer. Praise God for making the wisdom of the world foolish and for choosing what is weak, foolish, and despised in the world to shame the wise and strong. Thank Him that you can boast in nothing but Christ. Thank Him that the message of the Cross is the power of God in your life.

1 CORINTHIANS 2:6-16

True Wisdom

Paul has deliberately made himself and the gospel sound foolish in order to debunk the Greek pride in human reasoning. Now Paul qualifies his rejection of wisdom: there is a wisdom he does teach.

Read 2:6-16 carefully, asking God to give you His mind to understand.

For Further Study:
What is "God's secret wisdom" (2:7) that Paul teaches only to the mature? Read his letter to the Ephesians.

1. Summarize the main point of this passage in a sentence or two.

_____

_____

_____

_____

_____

2. What do you think Paul means by saying that the rulers of this age "are coming to nothing" (2:6)?

_____

_____

_____

_____

_____

For Thought and Discussion: Does Paul mean in 2:10-16 that spiritual people don't need to study the Scriptures with any aids or human guidance because the Spirit will reveal all truth to them directly? Why or why not?

For Further Study: Research what the Bible says about the human spirit, using a concordance. Begin with 2:11. What does a person's spirit do? Is the spirit different from the soul? If so, how and to what extent is it different? What is the spirit?

Lord of glory (2:8). The Jews used this title only for God the Father.[1] "Of glory" means "whose essential attribute is glory."

Spirit of the world (2:12). This may mean Satan (compare John 12:31), but it more probably means "'the spirit of human wisdom', 'the temper of this [age]'."[2]

Expressing spiritual truths in spiritual words (2:13). Literally, "combining spiritual things with spiritual (things or people)." Most commentators think the NIV has rendered the sense of this phrase accurately.

Man without the Spirit (2:14). Literally, "soulish man" (Greek: *psychikos* from *psyche*, "soul"). "Soulish" means natural, not sinful. Animals are soulish creatures—in Genesis 1:22,24; 2:7, "living creatures" and "living being" are literally "living soul(s)." However, unlike animals, man has the capacity to have the Holy Spirit dwell in him so that he becomes *pneumatikos*, "spiritual." Every human being has a human spirit (1 Corinthians 2:11) and has the capacity to have the Holy Spirit in him, but only followers of Christ actually do have the Holy Spirit.

In 15:44-49, Paul returns to this distinction between the natural (*psychikos*) and the spiritual (*pneumatikos*). The first Adam and all those who are "in Adam" (15:22) are natural, while the last Adam (Christ) and all those who are "in Christ" are spiritual. At the resurrection, our bodies will take on the character our spirits have already received.

3. What do we know about God's wisdom from 2:6-16? (Observe especially how it differs from the wisdom of this age.)

_____

_____

_____

_____

4. Why wouldn't the rulers of this age have crucified the Lord if they had understood God's wisdom (2:8)?

_____

_____

_____

_____

_____

5. What can we learn about the Holy Spirit from 2:10-16?

_____

_____

_____

_____

_____

6. Why is it possible to understand God's wisdom only if His Spirit reveals it (2:10-16)?

_____

_____

_____

_____

_____

Discerned . . . judgment(s) (2:14-15). The verb *anakrino* occurs three times in 2:14-15 as well as three times in 4:3-4. It means to make a "preliminary examination prior to the main hearing. . . . It comes to mean 'to scrutinize', 'to examine', and so 'to judge of', 'to estimate'."[3] The final judgment, of course, belongs to God, but even preliminary evaluations are risky for humans.

For Further Study:
Paul has a lot to say about judgment in 1 Corinthians. Watch for the various kinds of judgment (*krino, anakrino, diakrino*) as you study further (4:3-5; 5:3-5; 11:17-18,29-31).

For Thought and Discussion: How might one misinterpret or take to an extreme the idea that "we have the mind of Christ" (2:16)?

7. What do you think Paul means by the following statements?

"The spiritual man makes judgments about all things, but he himself is not subject to any man's judgment" (2:15, compare 4:3-4).

_____

_____

_____

_____

_____

_____

"We have the mind of Christ" (2:16).

_____

_____

_____

_____

_____

Study Skill—Outlining
Some sort of outline or chart can be invaluable in keeping track of an author's train of thought. In lesson one you used a broad outline to see 1 Corinthians as a whole. That broad outline is a good start toward a more thorough one. At this point, you might start working on an outline that reflects each paragraph of the book. For instance, to outline the first two chapters, simply divide the chapters into paragraphs and give each one a title. Group the paragraphs under the main headings you titled in question 3 of lesson one. Your outline will look something like this:
(continued on page 43)

(continued from page 42)

1:1-9 _____

1:10–4:21 _____

   1:10-17 _____

     1:18–3:4 _____

       1:18-25 _____

       1:26-31 _____

     2:1-5 _____

     2:6-16 _____

     3:1-4 _____

Optional Application: Have you experienced the Spirit enabling you to understand God's wisdom and gifts (2:12)? If so, how have you experienced this, and how should this affect your actions? If not, what do you think you should do about this?

Optional Application: Do you have the mind of Christ, as Paul did (2:16)? How do you know? How should you act in light of this?

8. As a start toward a detailed outline, give titles to each of the paragraphs of 1:10–4:21 that you have studied so far. (Feel free to look back at lesson three as well as the book itself.)

1:10-17 _____

1:18-25 _____

1:26-31 _____

2:1-5 _____

2:6-16 _____

Study Skill—Application

Ask yourself these questions when looking for something in a passage to apply to yourself:

    Is there a *sin* for me to avoid?
    Is there a *promise* for me to act on?
    Is there an *example* for me to follow?
    Is there a *command* for me to obey?
    How can this passage increase my *knowledge* of the Lord (not just knowledge about Him), and how should I respond?

    You can remember these five questions using the acronym SPECK—Sin, Promise, Example, Command, Knowledge.

Your response

9. What one truth from 2:6-16 seems most personally relevant to you?

_____

_____

_____

_____

_____

10. How have you already observed this truth at
work in your life?

_____

_____

_____

_____

_____

11. How do you fall short or want to grow in this
area?

_____

_____

_____

_____

_____

12. What steps can you take to act on this desire?

_____

_____

_____

_____

_____

13. List any questions you have about 2:6-16.

_____

_____

_____

_____

For the group

Warm-up. Ask, "In common phraseology, what does it mean to be a spiritual person?" Spiritual has many connotations in our society, so it might be helpful to contrast the common usage with the way Paul uses the term in 2:6-16. The Corinthians thought of themselves as spiritual in the common Greek sense—they were aficionados of the lofty, intellectual, mystical things of the spiritual realm. Paul's idea is quite different.

Read aloud and summarize.

Questions. Verses 15-16 in particular are open to several interpretations, some of them misleading. "We have the mind of Christ" and "we are subject to no man's judgment" have been slogans of cults and individuals who accept no authority beyond their own opinions. But since Paul was rebuking a group of self-styled spiritual people who were taking just this position, we can be sure that he did not mean that any believer should follow his own opinions because he has the mind of Christ. It is up to you to come up with a sound, consistent interpretation of these verses that takes into account all that Paul has to say about judgment, spirituality, and maturity. Don't worry if you don't exhaust the subject in one meeting; you'll be coming back to it in later lessons.

It might be helpful to make a chart contrasting the spiritual with the unspiritual (natural, soulish) person. However, in lesson five you'll be contrasting the spiritual, soulish, and worldly (carnal, fleshly) persons, so you might want to wait until then.

Plan a few minutes to share any questions or results from your applications of lesson three. Then discuss your applications for this lesson.

45

Summarize and wrap-up.

Prayer. Ask God to give each of you the mind of Christ and the indwelling teaching of the Holy Spirit. Ask Him to draw you on toward maturity in Christ so that you can understand the deep things of God revealed by the Spirit to the mature. Praise God for keeping His wisdom secret so that the rulers of this age would be confounded and His purpose would be accomplished. Thank Him for revealing His secrets to those who are indwelt by the Spirit.

1. Morris, page 56.
2. Morris, page 58.
3. Morris, page 60.

1 CORINTHIANS 3:1-23

Fleshly and Spiritual Attitudes

Some of the Corinthians disdain Paul because his preaching contains none of the sophisticated rhetoric and up-to-date wisdom they admire. But Paul disdains worldly wisdom and claims to possess a divine wisdom that he has not seen fit to share with the Corinthians. Now he goes on to set them straight about the attitudes they simply must grasp before they can even begin to comprehend God's wisdom.

Read 3:1-23, looking for these attitudes.

1. In one sentence each, summarize the main point of each paragraph in this chapter.

    3:1-4 _____

    _____

    3:5-9 _____

    _____

    3:10-15 _____

    _____

    3:16-17 _____

    _____

    3:18-23 _____

    _____

Spiritual or worldly (3:1-4)

Worldly (3:1,3). In 3:1 the word (*sarkinos*) means "made of flesh." When Paul was first in Corinth, the believers were new converts, **infants in Christ**. Although reborn by the Spirit, they were naturally still made of flesh, so Paul gave them **milk, not solid food** (3:2). He did not blame them for their infancy; it was expected.

Now, however, he does blame them. In 3:3 he shifts to the word *sarkikos*, which means "characterized by flesh." *Flesh* in Paul's terminology is the opposite of "Spirit." It seldom refers to the physical body, but rather to "fallen humanity with the sum-total of sinful propensities inherited by natural birth."[1] When the Corinthians were newborn, it was reasonable for them to still be made of flesh, but after years of supposed growth, it is shocking that they are still behaving like people characterized by flesh. They should be *pneumatikos*, behaving like people characterized by the Spirit.

2. Paul contrasts the spiritual, the natural, and the worldly persons in 2:12-3:4. Write down the characteristics of each.

spiritual/mature (2:6)
natural/soulish (2:14)
worldly/fleshly (3:1)

3. Do the Corinthian Christians have the Holy
   Spirit inside them? How do you know (1:4-7)?

   _____

   _____

   _____

   _____

   _____

**Optional
Application:** Are you
more like the spiritual
or the worldly person
you described in
question 2? What can
you do about this?

4. Are they behaving as spiritual people? Explain.

   _____

   _____

   _____

   _____

   _____

5. So, in what sense are the Corinthians spiritual
   and in what sense are they not?

   _____

   _____

   _____

   _____

   _____

6. What can we conclude about what it means to
   be spiritual? (For example: Can you be soulish
   and spiritual? Can you be fleshly *and* spiritual?
   Why or why not?)

   _____

   _____

   _____

   _____

   _____

   _____

**Optional
Application:** How
should your attitudes
and actions be
affected by the fact
that your church or
fellowship as a group
is the temple of the
Holy Spirit?

Building the church (3:5-17)

7. Why are factional divisions evidence that a
group of people is worldly and unable to understand God's wisdom (3:5-9)?

_____

_____

_____

_____

_____

Rewarded (3:8,14). The Greek word refers to a wage
for work done.[2] Notice that the wage is for
labor, not results, and that the wage is not salvation (which is a free gift) but something
further that the Scriptures do not fully explain
(but see Matthew 25:14-30, Luke 19:11-27).

Expert builder (3:10). An *architektōn* "was the
man who superintended the work of building,"[3]
the foreman. Paul saw his own commission as
being to lay the foundations of churches; he left
the further construction to others. (Observe this
pattern in the book of Acts.)

You (3:16). This word is plural in Greek. Paul is
speaking to the believers in Corinth as a group.
In 6:19, he says the same thing about each
believer as an individual.

8. In 3:5-9, Paul compares the church (the people)
to a field and himself to a farmworker. In
3:9-17, he switches to the imagery of a building.

a. Who is the building (3:9)?

_____

b. What kind of building are they, and what are
some of the implications of this (3:16)?

_____

_____

_____

_____

_____

c. Who are those who build on the foundation?

_____

_____

d. How does Paul warn a person to build?

foundation _____

_____

_____

construction _____

_____

_____

e. What does Paul mean by . . .

gold, silver, and costly stones? _____

_____

_____

wood, hay, and straw? _____

_____

_____

f. What happens to a person if he builds with the wrong materials (3:13-15)? (Does he lose his salvation? Explain.)

_____

_____

_____

_____

For Thought and Discussion: Do you think 3:10-17 applies only to Christian teachers or to every Christian? Do all, or only some, have responsibilities for building the church? Explain your reasoning.

51

Optional Application: How is 3:10-15 relevant to the way you spend your time and energy?

For Thought and Discussion: How would factionalism and worldly wisdom be either strawy material or actually destroy the building?

9. Summarize the point Paul is making in 3:10-15.

_____

_____

_____

_____

_____

10. In contrast to the poor builder (3:10-15), one who actually destroys the building will be destroyed (3:17). How would someone destroy the building?

_____

_____

_____

_____

All things are yours (3:18-23)

11. The whole debate about Paul versus Apollos is an example of worldly wisdom that should be abandoned (3:18-21). In light of 3:10-17, why should a person abandon the world's wisdom?

_____

_____

_____

_____

12. a. What does Paul mean by saying "all things are yours" (3:21)?

_____

_____

_____

_____

b. How is this relevant to the topic at hand—
the rebuke for boasting about various leaders?

_____

_____

_____

_____

_____

For Thought and Discussion: a. What does it mean that we are "of Christ" (3:23)? What are the implications for our attitudes and actions?

b. In what sense is Christ "of God"? Does He belong to God in the same way we belong to Christ? Explain. (See 15:23-28.)

Your response

13. What one insight from 3:1-23 would you like to take to heart this week?

_____

_____

_____

_____

14. How would you like this truth to affect your life in deeper ways?

_____

_____

_____

_____

_____

15. What steps can you take to cooperate with God in bringing this about?

_____

_____

_____

_____

_____

16. List any questions you have about chapter 3.

_____

_____

_____

_____

For the group

Warm-up. Ask everyone to think about this question for a moment and then answer it briefly: "What have you done this week to help build up God's church in some way?"

Questions. This is a long lesson, so you may want to focus either on the contrast among spiritual, worldly, and soulish, or on the imagery of building. As always, urge the group to plan specific, active applications.

Prayer. Ask God to make each of you more spiritual and mature. Ask Him to show you any ways in which you are boasting about one leader or denigrating another. Praise Him for making you part of His field and His temple. Thank Him for making all things yours and for making you Christ's. Once again, praise Him for confounding the worldly wise. If it seems appropriate, take time to pray for guidance about how you (as a group or as individuals) can participate in building up the church in deeper ways.

1. Bruce, *1 and 2 Corinthians*, page 42.
2. Morris, page 65.
3. Morris, page 66.

LESSON SIX

1 CORINTHIANS 4:1-21

Apostles of Christ

At the root of the Corinthians' squabbling over which leader is best lies a distorted idea of the Christian message, of Christian ministry and ministers, and of the Christian life. The Corinthians think the message should seem wise by worldly standards, but in fact it seems foolish. As for the lives of Christian leaders and people, read 4:1-21.

For Further Study:
What are "the secret things of God" (4:1)? (See, for example, Romans 11:25, Ephesians 3:2-6, Colossians 1:25-27.)

Judgment (4:1-5)

Those entrusted (4:1). The Greek word means "manager" or "steward." The owner of a large estate usually put one slave in charge of all the estate's affairs and its other slaves. This manager was a slave to his master but an overseer to the other slaves.

Judge (4:3-5). The word in 4:3-4 is *anakrino*, a preliminary judgment or cross-examination. In 4:5 it is *krino*, a final judgment.

1. Instead of putting leaders on pedestals and boasting about some and criticizing others, how should Christians regard their leaders (4:1)?

_____

_____

55

For Further Study:
Study what the New Testament teaches about judging, finding consistent principles. Who is qualified to make judgments about things, people, etc.? Who is not? What are the various kinds of judgments—discernment, evaluation, discrimination, condemnation? Which of these should we make, and which should we not make? Begin with Matthew 7:1-5,15-20; Romans 2:11-16; 1 Corinthians 2:14-16; 4:3-5; 5:1-5,12-13; 6:1-6; 11:28-32; and 1 John 4:1-3.

_____

_____

2. Since this is who Christian leaders really are, what attitudes should the leaders have?

4:2 _____

_____

_____

4:3-4 _____

_____

_____

3. Why don't Christians need to judge each other's—or their own—performance regarding their service to God (4:5)?

_____

_____

_____

4. Does this mean we can be indifferent about how well we serve God? Why or why not? (Consider 3:10-15.)

_____

_____

_____

_____

5. In practice, how can you go about not judging yourself (4:3-4), while at the same time being careful how you build (3:10)?

_____

_____

_____

_____

Kings and spectacles (4:6-21)

Take pride (4:6). Literally, "be inflated" or "be puffed up." This verb appears six times in this letter (4:18-19, 5:2, 8:1, 13:4) but only once elsewhere in Paul's epistles. He evidently thought it was especially relevant to the Corinthians. *Boast* is another verb that occurs frequently (1:29,31; 3:21; 4:7).

6. How were the Corinthians going beyond the teaching of Scripture in their behavior and attitudes (4:6)? (*Optional:* See Proverbs 16:18, 29:23; Jeremiah 9:23-24.)

_____

_____

_____

_____

Already (4:8). Paul taught that Christ has been raised from death and is now reigning in glory (15:25). When He returns, we will rise from death and share that reign (15:22-23). But just as suffering preceded glory for Him, so it will be for us (Romans 8:17, 2 Timothy 2:12). However, some of the Corinthians "were speaking and acting as if they had already attained the kingdom and the glory simultaneously with the gift of the Spirit."[1] In 1 Corinthians 15:12, 2 Thessalonians 2:2, and 2 Timothy 2:18, we hear about teachers who were claiming that the resurrection and the day of the Lord had already taken place.

Stoicism, a philosophical system popular in that day, fed this idea. Self-sufficiency was the great Stoic virtue, and Stoics believed that you are what you think. This was a Stoic slogan, "I alone am rich, I alone reign as king."[2]

Spectacle (4:9). Literally, "theater." It was customary to have a procession to the arena for the gladiatorial games. The doomed gladiators and

For Thought and Discussion: "Puffed up" is a colorful word to depict pride. Why is it appropriate to portray a proud person as inflated?

For Further Study: Compare the Corinthians' attitude in 4:8 to Jesus' teaching in Matthew 5:6 and Revelation 3:17. How is all this relevant to you?

57

For Further Study:
First Corinthians
4:11-13 describes
Paul's situation in
Ephesus during his
work there. For more
on this period of his
life, read Acts
19:1-41.

**For Thought and
Discussion:** a. How
did Paul become the
Corinthians' father in
Christ (4:15)?
b. How should
this affect the way
they treat him?
c. To what extent
does this apply to
Christians today
whose spiritual
parents are not
apostles?

**For Thought and
Discussion:** a. Is it
arrogant for Paul to
say "imitate me"
(4:16)? Why or
why not?
b. Would it be
arrogant for you to
say this? Why or
why not?
c. How should
this affect your
actions?

men condemned to die by being thrown to the
beasts were led at the end of the procession so
that the crowd could gape and jeer at them.[3]

7. Why shouldn't the Corinthians be proud?

4:7 _____

_____

_____

4:8-13 _____

_____

_____

_____

8. We learned something about what it means to
be an apostle from 4:1-5. What can we learn
about an apostle's life and calling from 4:8-16?

_____

_____

_____

_____

_____

9. What lessons for your life does this description
offer?

_____

_____

_____

_____

_____

Timothy (4:17). He was a younger member of Paul's mission team. He had become a Christian in response to Paul's preaching, then later joined his team in time to participate in the missions to Philippi, Thessalonica, Corinth, and Ephesus. Paul was in the habit of sending his colleagues back to churches he had founded for checkup visits, and Timothy was one of his favorite emissaries (Acts 16:1-19:22, Philippians 2:19-23).

For Further Study:
Use a concordance to find references to the Kingdom of God. What do you learn about it?

10. Paul gets firm with the arrogant members of the Corinthian church who are denigrating his authority (4:18-21). What does he mean by saying "the kingdom of God is not a matter of talk but of power" (4:20)?

a. What is the Kingdom of God? (*Optional:* See Luke 4:18-19,38-44; 11:14-20; 17:20-21.)

_____

_____

_____

_____

b. How is the Kingdom a matter of power?

_____

_____

_____

_____

c. In what ways is this truth relevant to your life?

_____

_____

_____

_____

59

For Further Study:
Add 4:1-21 to your
outline of 1 Corinthi-
ans. Decide on a title
for each paragraph
that you think
expresses its content.

11. Having examined all of Paul's words on the sub-
    ject, summarize why Christians should not
    divide into factions and exalt certain leaders
    over the rest (1:10-4:21).

    _____

    _____

    _____

    _____

    _____

    _____

    _____

    _____

Your response

12. What one insight from chapter 4 would you like
    to concentrate on for application?

    _____

    _____

    _____

    _____

    _____

13. How would you like this insight to influence
    your life more deeply?

    _____

    _____

    _____

    _____

    _____

    _____

14. What can you do to put this into practice, with God's help?

_____

_____

_____

_____

_____

15. List any questions you have about 4:1-21.

_____

_____

_____

_____

For the group

Warm-up. Ask group members how they would describe their Christian life—as easy, tough, challenging, glorious, frustrating, etc.

Questions. Paul speaks of his apostolic office in this chapter, but he explicitly says that he does so in order that we may learn from the apostles' example. How closely do you think your lives should conform to the portrait Paul paints of his own in 4:1-5,8-13? How does his instruction to "imitate me" (4:16) apply to each of you?

Prayer. It is easy to feel that we fall far short of the standard Paul sets in this chapter. Pray for each other to be able to imitate Paul in his attitudes and priorities. Ask God to make the power of the Kingdom active in your lives. Praise Him that He alone is worthy to judge you and your fellow Christians. Thank Him for the mission and the models He has given you.

1. Bruce, *1 and 2 Corinthians*, page 49.
2. Morris, page 79.
3. Morris, page 80.

1 CORINTHIANS 5:1-13

Dealing with Immorality

The Corinthians have been displaying their arrogance by splitting into factions over different Christian leaders. Sadly, this is not their worst evidence of pride. Read 5:1-13.

Incest (5:1-5)

Sexual immorality (5:1). *Porneia* originally meant consorting with a prostitute, but it came to refer to any kind of sexual evil.[1] Here, it refers to incest—cohabitation within degrees forbidden by the Law of Moses (Leviticus 18:8; Deuteronomy 22:30, 27:20). The Greeks and Romans were notoriously lax about sexual ethics, but even they drew the line at incest. The Roman orator Cicero said of one such union that it was "incredible and, apart from this one instance, unheard of."[2]

His father's wife (5:1). Had this been the man's mother, Paul would probably have said so. She was probably his step-mother, but it is not clear whether his father was still alive, nor whether the man had married the step-mother or was simply living with her.

Proud (5:2). "Puffed up." From 6:12-20, it seems that a significant part of the church felt that as spiritual people they were no longer bound by

63

the rules that confined natural men. The idea that deeds of the body were morally neutral for men led by the spirit was popular among several pagan cults, and apparently it had infected this Christian group. To these Corinthians, liberty in Christ meant liberation from everything dictated in the Jewish Law and license to do things that shocked even pagans. Paul views this pride in false liberty as even more obscene than the sexual sin itself.[3]

Sinful nature (5:5). Literally, "flesh." The phrase "for the destruction of his flesh" (NASB) could mean that being cast out of the church will bring the man to such anguish that he will repent and God will slay his sinful nature. Or, it could mean that being expelled from the spiritual protection of the church body into Satan's domain will subject the man to sickness or even death—the destruction of the physical flesh. (See Acts 5:1-6, 1 Corinthians 11:30.)

1. Explain in general how the church should react to gross sin being practiced by an unrepentant member (5:1-5).

_____

_____

_____

_____

2. What do you think Paul means by each of these phrases?

"when you are assembled in the name of our Lord Jesus and I am with you in spirit" (5:4)

_____

_____

_____

_____

_____

64

"the power of our Lord Jesus is present" (5:4)

_____

_____

_____

_____

_____

"hand this man over to Satan" (5:5)

_____

_____

_____

_____

_____

"for the destruction of his flesh, that his spirit may be saved" (5:5, NASB)

_____

_____

_____

_____

_____

3. Is this procedure applicable in your church or fellowship? If so, how, and in what circumstances? If not, why not?

_____

_____

_____

_____

_____

For Thought and Discussion: What are some of the complicating factors in applying 5:1-5 today?

For Further Study:
a. Study the use and symbolism of yeast (leaven) in Scripture.
   b. Research the meaning of Passover, and how it figures in both the Old and the New Testaments.

Yeast (5:6-8)

Passover lamb (5:7). Passover celebrated Israel's exodus from Egypt. God sent a curse to kill all the firstborn in Egypt, but He told the Israelites to slaughter lambs (or goats), smear the blood on the doorposts of their houses to mark the homes that should not be cursed, and eat the lambs. Each year, the Jews sacrificed lambs and ate the meat in a meal that commemorated their deliverance from slavery (Exodus 12:1-13). In His death on the very eve of Passover, Christ fulfilled the true meaning of the Passover sacrifice, liberating from slavery to sin all those who put their faith in Him (Isaiah 53:4-7, John 1:29).

On the day before the Passover sacrifice and meal, the Jews were supposed to remove all the yeast (leaven) and leavened bread from their houses. For Passover and seven days thereafter, they were supposed to eat only unleavened bread as a sign of their purity (Exodus 12:14-20). Yeast symbolized defilement. It was unthinkable that the Passover lamb had already been sacrificed yet there was still yeast among the believers.

Sincerity and truth (5:8). "Purity of motive" and "purity of action."[4]

4. To what "boasting" is Paul referring in 5:6? What are the Corinthians boasting about?

_____

_____

_____

_____

5. Why is their boasting bad? (Explain the figure of speech in 5:6.)

_____

_____

66

6. a. What does it mean that Christians "really are" bread without yeast (5:7)?

_____

_____

_____

_____

_____

b. How should this affect our behavior?

_____

_____

_____

_____

For Further Study:
a. Research Jesus' practice on associating and eating with sinners, and His reasons for His policy (such as Luke 5:27-32, 7:33-35).
b. How should Jesus' and Paul's teaching and example apply to the situations you face?

For Thought and Discussion: To what extent do you think people should be expected to clean up their lives before joining the church, and why? Support your view from Scripture.

Shun false brothers (5:9-13)

I have written (5:9). In a previous letter (now lost), Paul apparently told the Corinthians not to associate with flagrant sinners, and they interpreted him to mean nonChristians who were flagrant sinners. Now he clarifies his meaning.

7. With what seriously immoral people may a Christian associate, and why (5:9-10,12-13)?

_____

_____

_____

_____

_____

For Thought and Discussion: Do you know any Christians who are greedy, slanderers, etc.? How do you treat them? How should you treat them?

Optional Application: Do you practice any of the sins Paul names in 5:11? If so, confess and commit yourself to change with God's help. What steps can you take?

For Further Study: Add chapter 5 to your outline of 1 Corinthians.

8. With what grossly immoral people may a Christian neither associate nor even eat, and why (5:6,11-13)?

_____

_____

_____

_____

_____

9. What does each of the following sins involve (use a dictionary if necessary), and why is each on the level of sexual immorality and idolatry?

greed (NASB: covetousness) _____

_____

_____

_____

_____

_____

slander (NASB: reviling) _____

_____

_____

_____

_____

Your response

10. In a sentence, summarize the main point Paul makes in 5:1-13.

_____

_____

_____

_____

_____

11. What aspect of 5:1-13 would you like to take to
    heart?

_____

_____

_____

_____

_____

12. How do you fall short in this area? How would
    you like this truth to affect your life more
    deeply?

_____

_____

_____

_____

_____

13. What action can you take along these lines,
    with God's help?

_____

_____

_____

_____

_____

14. List any questions you have about chapter 5.

_____

_____

_____

_____

For the group

Warm-up. How to apply this chapter is a subject of sometimes heated debate. It may be helpful to let group members air their feelings before you examine the text. Feelings are often not the best guides to action, and they are less likely to cloud group members' judgments and subvert your discussion if you let everyone express them. So, before even reading the passage, ask everyone, "Are there any sins that a professing Christian could practice that would make you refuse to associate with him or her? If so, what are those sins? If not, why not?" Since there have been legal cases against churches who have denounced and expelled members for sin, this question may provoke some impassioned responses on both sides. Don't let people start debating the issue now, just let them express themselves briefly.

Go around the room and ask for an initial gut-feeling response to the warm-up question. Emphasize that at this point you only want to know how people feel, and that later you will explore together the biblical teaching on this subject. Of course, it's okay for people to say they aren't sure how they feel about the issue.

Questions. When you think you all understand what Paul says and his reasons for his teaching, take a good chunk of time to discuss how his words apply to you and the groups you belong to. What are some of the dangers and complications of trying to do what Paul describes? How would you go about doing what Paul says while maintaining Jesus' attitude of love and welcome to sinners?

Prayer. Without mentioning names or specifics, pray for anyone you know who is in the grip of severe sin. Ask the Lord to protect each of you from the sins Paul names. Ask Him to give you and the groups you are involved with wisdom to deal with members and nonmembers who are practicing flagrant, unrepentant sin. Thank Him for Christ, your Passover Lamb, and for making you a new batch of dough without the yeast of malice and wickedness.

1. Morris, page 86.
2. Bruce, *1 and 2 Corinthians*, page 53.
3. Bruce, *1 and 2 Corinthians*, page 54.
4. Morris, page 90.

1 CORINTHIANS 6:1-20

More Moral Laxity

Paul tells the Corinthians that his performance as an apostle is not subject to the judgment of any man, least of all people who by their boasting and pride have shown themselves to be spiritually immature (3:14-16, 4:3-5). But judgments regarding moral behavior are another matter. Paul not only accepts, he demands that the Corinthians judge members who commit flagrant sin and thereby defile the reputation of the whole Body of Christ (5:1-13). This reminds Paul of another piece of news he has heard: while refusing to judge sin in their midst, the Corinthians are actually seeking judgments from unbelievers! Read 6:1-20, observing how this chapter is connected to the previous one.

Lawsuits (6:1-11)

Dispute (6:1). Verse 7 suggests that property cases or other civil suits are in view here. Criminal cases were required to be handled by the state (Romans 13:3-4), but Roman law allowed the Jews to apply their own laws in civil matters. Christians had the same rights because Rome still viewed them as a sect within Judaism.[1]

Ungodly (6:1). Paul is not saying that the judges in pagan courts are unjust, merely that they are not made righteous before God through faith in Christ.

Even men of little account (6:4). The Greek could mean that even the lowliest members of the church would be more acceptable judges for Christians than pagan courts. Or, Paul may be asking ironically if believers should be submitting their cases to pagans, who have no standing in the church and so are not really qualified to judge its members.

1. Paul has been talking about judging those inside and outside the church. What has been his teaching in this area so far?

2:15–3:4 _____

_____

_____

_____

3:10 _____

_____

_____

3:19 _____

_____

_____

_____

4:1-5 _____

_____

_____

_____

_____

5:1-5 _____

_____

_____

_____

5:9-13 _____

_____

_____

_____

_____

For Thought and Discussion: How do you and other members of your church or fellowship go about settling disputes? How do you think you should do so?

2. In 6:1-6, Paul is talking not about judging someone's behavior, but about judging between two parties in a dispute. What is his basic point?

_____

_____

_____

_____

_____

For Thought and Discussion: Why is it scandalous that Christians are taking each other to court in front of unbelievers (6:2-6)?

3. In support of his thesis, Paul makes some amazing statements as though they should be common knowledge to his readers. What do you think the following mean?

"The saints will judge the world" (6:2). (*Optional:* See Matthew 19:28, 2 Timothy 2:12, Revelation 20:4.)

_____

_____

_____

_____

"We will judge angels" (6:3). (*Optional:* See Jude 6.)

_____

_____

_____

_____

For Thought and Discussion: a. If a Christian today feels he has been cheated by another Christian, what do you think he should do? (Consider 5:11, 6:1-11.)

b. What do you think he should do if the one he accuses is unwilling to submit to the judgment of some particular body of believers?

For Further Study: Study Jesus' teaching from which Paul probably derives 1 Corinthians 6:7 (Luke 6:27-38). How do you think you should apply this teaching?

For Thought and Discussion: Christian A has cheated Christian B with the confidence that B would not dare take A to court. How would you deal with A in a biblical fashion?

4. Why does having lawsuits prove that the Corinthians have been "completely defeated"?

6:7 _____

_____

_____

_____

6:8-11 _____

_____

_____

_____

Washed . . . sanctified . . . justified (6:11). Cleansed from the guilt and defilement of sin, set apart as God's holy people, and declared "not guilty" in God's court of law.

Immorality (6:12-20)

Having dealt with the matter of lawsuits, Paul returns to the Corinthians' misguided attitudes about sexual morality.

Everything is permissible for me (6:12). This was apparently a slogan of one of the Corinthian parties. It appears this faction felt that they were reigning with Christ already (4:8) and that they were liberated from the Law because (as a group of heretical Christians in Rome put it a few decades later) "for a king there is no law prescribed." That later group cited Matthew 17:25-26 as proof that they could do as they pleased, and the Corinthians may have been thinking along similar lines.[2] Paul would never side with the legalists and deny the believers' freedom in Christ, but neither could he countenance the extreme position of the libertines.

Food for the stomach and the stomach for food
(6:13). Both Jesus and Paul taught that the physical act of eating and digesting is morally neutral and does not affect a person's inner spiritual state (Matthew 15:10-20, Romans 14:14). The view of the libertine Corinthians was that sexual acts were in the same category: what the body did had no effect on the spirit. In this they were reflecting the common view of their day in a town where cult prostitution was a thriving enterprise.

5. What reasons does Paul give for not having sex outside marriage?

6:12a _____

_____

_____

6:12b _____

_____

_____

6:13-17 _____

_____

_____

_____

_____

6:18 _____

_____

_____

6:19-20 _____

_____

_____

_____

Optional Application: Why should 6:11 motivate you to utterly turn from greed, cheating, sexual sin, slander, and all other sin? Meditate on these truths this week, and remind yourself of them when you are tempted to sin.

For Thought and Discussion: How does uniting with someone sexually affect a person afterward (6:16-17)? Can you explain this from your own or others' experience?

For Thought and Discussion: What does it mean to be one with a prostitute in body (6:16)? What does it mean to be one with Christ in spirit (6:17)? Is it possible to be one with both? Why or why not?

For Thought and Discussion: a. How do 3:16 and 6:19 complement each other?

b. How should each affect your conduct?

Optional Application: Think of some pleasure you are fond of. Evaluate it according to the tests in 6:12-13,19-20.

Is it beneficial?

Is it threatening to control you?

Does it glorify God, who has bought you at a price and made your body His temple?

6. Would you say that Paul thinks physical bodies are evil or base? What does he say about bodies and their value (6:12-20)?

7. How should these truths about the body affect your attitudes and practices?

Your response

8. What one insight from 6:1-20 would you like to apply to your own life?

9. How have you already seen this truth at work in your life?

10. What further effects would you like it to have on you?

_____

_____

_____

_____

_____

11. What steps can you take along these lines?

_____

_____

_____

_____

_____

12. List any questions you have about 6:1-20.

_____

_____

_____

_____

_____

For Thought and Discussion: With what price have you been purchased (6:20)? See 1 Peter 1:18-19.

For Further Study: Add chapter 6 to your outline.

For the group

Warm-up. Modern people share many of the same attitudes about bodies that people had in Paul's day. There are those who feel they can do anything to and with their bodies because they basically value them very little. Then, there are those who are extremely strict with and uncomfortable about bodies; these people are strongly negative about them. Again, there are those who pamper their bodies and derive much of their identity from them. None of these groups has God's view, which Paul states in 6:12-20.

Because these warped attitudes lie at the root of much of the abuse and indulgence of bodies in our culture, you might open this session by asking group members to tell briefly how they feel about their own bodies. "Do you like your body? Do you wish the Lord had given you a different one? Do you think you treat your body as it should be treated?" Let the group think about these questions for a minute or two, then ask for some responses. Leave the questions at the back of everyone's mind as you discuss what Paul has to say.

Questions. To some extent, 6:1-11 and 6:12-20 are distinct topics. You may choose to concentrate on one or to divide your time equally between both. Be sure to draw attention to and discuss the meaning of the statements about who you are:

"The saints will judge the world" (6:2);

"We will judge angels" (6:3);

Some of you were gross sinners, but "you were washed, you were sanctified, you were justified in the name of the Lord Jesus Christ and by the Spirit of our God" (6:11);

"Your bodies are members of Christ himself" (6:15);

"Your body is a temple of the Holy Spirit" (6:19);

"You are not your own; you were bought with a price" (6:19-20).

What implications does each of these astounding affirmations have for your lives? Why should these motivate you to abandon the kinds of sins Paul discusses in chapter 6, as well as others that tempt you?

Prayer. Thank God for the amazing things He says about you in this chapter. Thank Him for the promises He has made: to raise you bodily from death, to make you a judge over the world and even angels, to unite you with His Son. Thank Him for what He has already done for you: bought you with the blood of Jesus, washed you, justified you, sanctified you, made you a temple of the Holy Spirit. Ask Him to enable each of you to live in the light of these great truths.

1. Bruce, *1 and 2 Corinthians*, page 59.
2. Bruce, *1 and 2 Corinthians*, pages 49-50.

1 CORINTHIANS 7:1-40

Marriage

Paul has responded to the news about factions brought by Chloe's people and to other reports of sexual immorality and lawsuits among the believers in Corinth. Several of the factions are hostile to Paul, but at least some of the Corinthians respect him and want to know what he thinks on some issues they are facing. They have sent Stephanas, Fortunatus, and Achaicus (16:17) with a letter containing their questions. For much of the rest of this epistle, Paul replies to those questions.

Read 7:1-40, trying to deduce what question Paul has been asked and to grasp his point of view.

1. Overall, how would you describe Paul's view of marriage in 7:1-40?

_____

_____

_____

_____

_____

A little background might help you understand why Paul says what he says. In chapter 6 he was replying to one group who felt that sexual behavior was morally indifferent; to them he emphasized the ethical seriousness of sex. But side by side with those who regarded sex as neutral were those who considered

For Further Study:
a. Research all of
Paul's teaching on
marriage, beginning
with Ephesians
5:21-33.
    b. Study what
Jesus Christ and
biblical authors
say about marriage
and sex.

it base. The Greeks considered spirit good and matter evil. Thus, the human spirit was divine but the body was corrupt. Some people concluded that a spiritual person could therefore do anything he liked with his body, while others concluded that a spiritual person should deny his body's desires, especially those for food and sex. These same two pagan points of view were apparently rife in the Corinthian church. Paul responded to the first in chapter 6; he addresses the second in chapter 7. Some members of the church were evidently saying that Christians should avoid not only sex outside marriage, but also sex inside marriage, and even marriage itself. Since Paul was himself unmarried and celibate, they pointed to him as an example of the truly spiritual man. In reply, Paul explains why he recommends his own lifestyle to those who can handle it, but unhesitantly advises marriage to everyone else.

Not I, but the Lord (7:10). During His earthly ministry, Jesus gave explicit commands that married couples should stay married (Matthew 5:32, 19:3-9; Mark 10:2-12; Luke 16:18). When such direct words of Jesus were available, an apostle would quote them. However, when Jesus had not explicitly addressed an issue, an apostle gave his own judgment, making it clear that it was his own (7:12,25,40). It was his personal view, but he underscored his authority by saying ***I give a judgment as one who by the Lord's mercy is trustworthy*** (7:25) and ***I think that I too have the Spirit of God*** (7:40).

Sanctified (7:14). A new believer is not less set apart for God because he or she is married to an unbeliever. Rather, the unbeliever is in some sense set apart for God because he or she is married to a believer. "It is not possible to give precise definition of what this signifies. But it is a scriptural principle that the blessings arising from fellowship with God are not confined to the immediate recipients, but extend to others" (Genesis 17:7, 18:26-28; 1 Kings 15:4).[1]

Virgin (7:36). In Paul's day, parents and guardians had the biggest say in whether a woman could

80

marry. So, in 7:36-38 Paul may be addressing the decision of Christian parents and guardians as to whether they should give their daughters in marriage. Or it may be that Paul is speaking to Christian men deciding whether to marry their fiancées.

2. Outline chapter 7 by writing down what issue Paul addresses in each paragraph.

7:1-7 _____

_____

7:8-9 _____

_____

7:10-11 _____

_____

7:12-16 _____

_____

7:17-24 _____

_____

7:25-35 _____

_____

7:36-38 _____

_____

7:39-40 _____

_____

3. In each of the following passages, whom does Paul advise to marry, and why?

7:8-9 _____

_____

_____

For Thought and Discussion: What does it mean to "fulfill his marital duty" (7:3)?

For Thought and Discussion: Why does temporary abstinence help a person devote himself or herself to prayer (7:5)?

7:36-38 _____

_____

_____

4. What does Paul teach about married couples in these verses? (Explain in your own words.)

7:1-7 _____

_____

_____

_____

_____

_____

_____

7:10-11 _____

_____

_____

_____

7:39 _____

_____

_____

_____

5. a. Read Paul's policy on becoming divorced from an unbelieving spouse (7:12-16). Why should you stay married to an unbeliever if he or she wants to do so (7:14-15)?

_____

_____

_____

_____

_____

b. Why should you allow the divorce if the unbeliever wants it (7:15-16)?

_____

_____

_____

For Thought and Discussion: What do you think Paul means by saying that the children of a believer are holy (7:14)?

For Thought and Discussion: Do you think "the present crisis" (7:26) applies to the situation now? Why or why not?

The present crisis (7:26). Paul may be speaking generally of the time up until Christ's return. All Christians are in a sense on active duty in a cosmic conflict between two kingdoms as they await the final cataclysm. The world is perpetually hostile to those who truly try to live the gospel (2 Timothy 3:12).

Or, he may be referring to an especially tough situation in Corinth, which was a hostile and immoral environment. In this latter case, Paul's inclination to refrain from marriage applies to such a crisis, but not to all times and situations.

6. In light of the present crisis and the shortness of the time, what general principle does Paul state repeatedly in 7:17,20,24,26?

_____

_____

_____

7. How does this principle apply to . . .

Jews and nonJews (7:17-19)? _____

_____

_____

_____

slaves (7:21)? _____

_____

_____

83

singles and married people (7:7-8,29,32-35)?

_____

_____

_____

8. How can "those who have wives . . . live as if they had none" (7:29)? What does this mean, and how should a person do this in practice?

_____

_____

_____

_____

_____

9. How can those who mourn or are happy live as if they were not (7:30)?

_____

_____

_____

_____

_____

_____

Your response

10. What implications does this teaching in 7:1-40 have for your life? What truth or truths would you like to take to heart?

_____

_____

_____

_____

_____

11. How would you like this to affect your priorities and actions?

_____

_____

_____

_____

_____

12. What steps do you think you should take during the next week or so along these lines?

_____

_____

_____

_____

_____

13. List any questions you have about 7:1-40.

_____

_____

_____

_____

For Further Study: Add chapter 7 to your outline of 1 Corinthians.

Optional Application: In light of 7:1-40, do you think Paul would advise you personally to be married or not? Why?

For the group

Warm-up. You might ask, "For you personally, do you think marriage makes (or would make) the Christian life easier or harder? Why?" Don't spend a lot of time on this; it is just a chance for everyone to express personal opinions before you dive into the text. Many people have strong opinions about Paul's views in chapter 7. You don't want the group to base actions on personal opinions apart from Scripture, and getting opinions out in the open helps to prevent this. Such a question may also help you get to know each other better.

Read aloud and summarize. Question 1 is a good opening summary question. Paul has sometimes been falsely represented as being against marriage and women in general. Your study should explode this myth.

Questions. Many of the numbered questions are purely observations from the text. You may want to spend most of your time discussing what Paul means by certain statements (such as that children of believers are holy, or that those who have wives should live as though they had none) and how what he says applies to you.

Wrap-up.

Prayer. Thank God for instituting marriage. Thank Him for calling some people to be married and some to be single. Ask Him to help each of you make decisions about whether and how to change your current marital, employment, and other states. Ask Him to enable you to live in light of the fact that the time is short, this world in its present form is passing away, and the things you have are not permanent. Ask Him to help you focus on pleasing Him in an undivided manner. Pray especially for any members of your group who are facing big decisions.

1. Morris, page 110.

1 CORINTHIANS 8:1-9:27

Freedom and Rights

We hear a lot about human rights and freedoms in our culture. Paul has taught the believers of Corinth that Christ has set them free, and some of them feel strongly about their rights as Christians. But what are our rights, and how should we use them? What does freedom in Christ entail? Paul's answers may surprise us. Read the whole of his counsel on this topic in 8:1-11:1.

1. What seems to have been the question the Corinthians were asking Paul (8:1)?

_____

_____

_____

_____

_____

Food from idols (8:1-13)

It was not easy to avoid meat sacrificed to idols in Corinth. For one thing, nearly all dinner parties, trade association meetings, and other social occasions included some dedication to the patron deity of the gathering. Many parties and meetings were actually held in temples.[1] Furthermore, nearly all butchers (except Jewish ones) sold sacrificed meat;

For Thought and Discussion: What common thread do you find in 1:21,27-29; 3:18-21; and 8:2? How does this theme apply to you?

many shops were even attached to temples. When an animal was offered in a temple, a small portion was burnt for the god, the worshipers got some (they usually ate it right there in a dinner party), and the priests got the rest. What the priests couldn't use they sold to the butchers. Since only the best animals could be offered to the gods, the best meat was more than likely from a sacrifice. So, in order to avoid idol meat, one would have to shop only at Jewish butchers (or Christian ones if there were any) and never attend any social occasions with pagans. For anyone whose livelihood depended in part on business dinners or trade association meetings, this was out of the question. For anyone who cared about his social standing, it was absurd.

Some of the Corinthian Christians reasoned that since the idols were not real gods, there was no reason to sabotage their businesses, their social standing, and their diets. These enlightened ones may have been the more wealthy and educated who were used to eating meat daily in ordinary, nonreligious situations. *Knowledge* was one of their great values.

However, others found it difficult to shake the idea that the idols they had been worshiping all their lives were not real, powerful entities who somehow contaminated the meat offered to them. Among this group were probably the poorer members of the church, whose daily diet was vegetarian and who normally saw meat only in temple feasts. For them, the association between meat and idolatry was strong. This group couldn't help feeling that by eating meat offered to idols they were defiling themselves, and by attending parties in temples they were countenancing the worship there.

There was one other factor in this debate. In the Jerusalem decree (Acts 15:29), the apostles had all agreed that the Gentiles need not be circumcised but must avoid sexual immorality and food sacrificed to idols. Paul did not mention this decree (to which he had agreed only a few years earlier) in his letter to Corinth, but some members of the church may have been trying to enforce it.

2. Paul agrees with the "strong" party that "we all possess knowledge" (8:1). What knowledge does Paul agree that "we" (that is, Paul and the strong ones) all possess (8:4-6)?

_____

_____

_____

_____

_____

_____

For Thought and Discussion: a. Does Paul scorn the weak brother in 8:9-13? Why or why not? (Consider 1:27-29.)
   b. How is this relevant to you?

3. If the knowledge "we" all possess were all there was to this issue of eating, then we could go ahead. However, what qualifies and limits this freedom?

8:1-3 _____

_____

_____

8:7-13 _____

_____

_____

_____

_____

_____

_____

4. Why does knowledge only puff up, but love builds up (8:1)?

_____

_____

_____

_____

_____

89

For Thought and Discussion: Why is it more important to be "known by God" (8:3) than to know about God, or even to know God (8:2)?

For Further Study: Regarding knowledge and love, see 1 John 4:8.

5. What does Paul mean in 8:2? (That is, why does thinking you know show that you don't know what you need to know?)

_____

_____

_____

_____

_____

_____

Paul's example (9:1-27)

Free (9:1). Free as all Christians are free. (The Corinthians had a high opinion of their freedom in Christ.)

Apostle (9:1). Because Paul had not followed Jesus during His earthly ministry, there were some who questioned his apostleship (Acts 1:21-26; 2 Corinthians 12:1-12; Galatians 1:1,15–2:10). Paul gives two proofs in 1 Corinthians 9:1-2 that he is a genuine apostle.

  Some members of the Apollos and Cephas factions in Corinth may have been saying that by not asking the believers to support himself and a wife for his work, Paul was acknowledging that he was inferior to the real apostles.

Seal (9:2). In a day when many people could not read, a signature was not a useful way to authenticate a document. Instead, people stamped distinctive marks into wax or clay to prove that a document was authentic.

Sit in judgment (9:3). "Examine" in NASB. This is the verb *anakrino* as in 2:14-15 and 4:3-4.

Is it about oxen that God is concerned? (9:9). Paul is not denying that God cares about oxen or that Deuteronomy 25:4 applies to oxen, but he is saying that the verse applies primarily to human workers. The verse occurs in a passage of the Law that is concerned with human activities.

To separate grain from chaff, it was customary to have oxen trample on it. When the trampled grain was then thrown in the breeze, the heavy kernels would fall to the ground, while the light chaff would blow away. God commanded Israel to let the oxen eat some of the grain while they worked.

6. What are the proofs that Paul is a genuine apostle (9:1-2)?

_____

_____

_____

_____

_____

_____

7. What rights of an apostle has he waived (9:3-6,12)?

_____

_____

_____

_____

_____

8. How does he defend the fact that he has these rights (9:7-11,13-14)?

_____

_____

_____

_____

_____

For Further Study: Read Paul's accounts of how he saw the Lord in Acts 9:1-9, 22:6-16, and 26:12-18.

For Thought and Discussion: a. What are some of your rights and freedoms as a Christian?

b. Under what circumstances are you free to use them, and under what circumstances should you not use them?

For Thought and Discussion: To whom among modern Christians does 9:7-12 apply? How does it apply? How should you act accordingly?

For Thought and Discussion: What does Paul mean by saying he preaches not voluntarily but under compulsion (9:16-17)?

For Thought and Discussion: What do you think a Christian should do if, in some situation, being all things to all men in order to save some (9:19-23) seems to contradict with not making a weak brother stumble (8:9-13)? That is, what should you do if your brother will be offended if you do a thing, and the unsaved person you are evangelizing will be offended if you don't? (Consider the apostles' decisions about food and cir-cumcision in Acts 15:19, Galatians 2:11-21.)

9. Why has Paul waived these rights?

9:12 _____

_____

9:15-18 _____

_____

_____

_____

10. a. According to 9:19-23, what other rights of a Christian is Paul not exercising?

_____

_____

_____

_____

_____

b. Why is he doing this?

_____

_____

_____

_____

_____

11. Describe one way in which the principles stated in 9:19 and 9:22 apply to your lifestyle among unbelievers.

_____

_____

_____

_____

_____

92

Race . . . games (9:24-25). The Corinthians were avid sports fans. The Isthmian games that their city sponsored attracted the best athletes in the Empire.

The verb rendered ***competes in the games*** is *agonizomai*, from which we get "agony" and "agonize." It was serious business. The ***strict training*** of a competitor in the Isthmian games lasted ten months. During this time, the athlete avoided not only sinful things, but even lawful ones that might hamper his effectiveness in any way. (NASB reads, "Everyone who competes in the games exercises self-control in all things.")

The victor's ***crown*** at the Isthmian games was a pine wreath.[2]

For Further Study:
a. What is the imperishable crown that a Christian laborer receives? Research the idea of crowns and rewards in the New Testament.

b. Does this conflict with the fact that salvation is a free gift? (See, for instance, 1 Corinthians 3:14-15.)

12. Why else does Paul not take advantage of all of his freedoms as a Christian (9:24-27)?

_____

_____

_____

_____

_____

13. In what ways do you need to be in "strict training" and making your body your slave (9:25,27) in order to win the imperishable prize?

_____

_____

_____

_____

_____

14. How is all this about Paul relevant to the topic of meat sacrificed to idols?

_____

_____

_____

_____

_____

Your response

15. What one aspect of 8:1-9:27 would you like to
    apply to your own life?

_____

_____

_____

_____

_____

16. How would you like this to affect your actions
    and attitudes?

_____

_____

_____

_____

_____

17. What steps can you take to begin putting this
    into practice more fully than you are?

_____

_____

_____

_____

_____

18. List any questions you have about 8:1-9:27.

_____

_____

94

_____

_____

For the group

Warm-up. Ask group members, "In any given situation, do you think you are more likely to do what you want, or what someone else wants?" You might also ask, "Do you think this is good or bad, and why?"

Questions. Chapters 8 and 9 are about asserting our rights and taking advantage of our freedom in Christ. Paul is scolding people who put their own preferences above everyone else's, whether fellow believers or the unsaved. Paul, by contrast, always puts the other person's needs first.

However, there are a lot of people who always put the other person's *wants* first in order to please everyone and avoid conflict. It is easy to confuse this doormat, appeasement attitude with the selflessness Paul is teaching. If you find that your group contains some people who are natural appeasers, you should ask some additional questions when you study the passage. What are Paul's motives in being "all things to all men"? Does he do this to earn their approval? From what you know of Paul in his other letters and the book of Acts, does he bend to what others want, or to what will advance the gospel? How are these different?

If, however, people in your group tend to do what they want, you might plan to examine why Paul often restricts his rights. What are some of your freedoms in Christ? Under what circumstances should you restrict them?

You might want to focus on just one or two issues. One might be the one described above. Another might be what you should do if the needs of the weak brother seem to conflict with the needs of the unsaved. A third might be how each of you should be in training, disciplining yourselves for the race.

Prayer. Thank God for all of your rights in Christ. Thank Him for putting you in the race for the crown that never fades, for giving each of you a job in His army. Thank Him for all of the other laborers whose work has benefited you. Praise Him for being the only God and the only Lord. Ask Him to show each of you how you should act in your various situations so that you cause no one to stumble and so that the unbelievers you encounter are attracted to the gospel.

1. Consider, for example, the "invitation cards" discovered among papyrus fragments in the Egyptian town of Oxyrhynchus. One of them reads, "Chaeremon invites you to dine at the table of the lord Sarapis at the Sarapeion [temple of Sarapis] tomorrow, the 15th, at the 9th hour." Or, consider the man in Bononia (Bologna) in Italy, who built a dining room dedicated to Jupiter Dolichenus, probably so that the god would be the patron of the parties there. See Bruce, *1 and 2 Corinthians*, page 81.
2. Morris, page 139.

1 CORINTHIANS 10:1-11:1

Freedom and Temptation

The Corinthians want to know what Paul thinks about eating meat that has been sacrificed to idols. One group ("the strong") feels they can eat anything because the idols are not really gods; the other ("the weak") still feels that idols have power. In response, Paul has agreed with the strong that their knowledge is accurate and their freedom valid, but he has pointed out that some things are more important than exercising such knowledge, freedom, and rights. For a whole chapter, Paul has discoursed on his personal policy regarding his rights. He ended chapter 9 with the alarming suggestion that if he did not voluntarily restrict his own rights, he might be disqualified for the prize offered to faithful workers.

The warning continues in chapter 10. As sympathetic as Paul is with those who know their freedom in Christ, he is adamant that they should understand the implications of freedom. Ask God to speak to you as you read chapter 10.

1. Paul is still explaining his views on eating idol meat. What is his basic point in each of the sections of chapter 10?

   10:1-13 _____

   _____

   _____

   _____

For Further Study:
To better understand the events Paul refers to in 10:1-10, read Exodus 13–17 and Numbers 10–15.

10:14-22 _____

_____

_____

_____

10:23-11:1 _____

_____

_____

_____

Israel's history

In chapter 9, Paul used his own life to illustrate his views on rights. Now he uses Old Testament events to further explain his attitudes on the subject of idol feasts.

Cloud . . . sea (10:1). During Israel's journey from Egypt to the Promised Land, God led the nation through the desert personally. He made His presence known by means of a cloud that shaded the people from the desert sun by day and became a pillar of fire to give them light by night (Exodus 13:17-22).

When Pharaoh changed his mind about freeing the Israelites and sent his army to pursue them, God opened a way in the Red Sea for His people to pass through but sent the waters crashing back to drown the Egyptians when they tried to follow (Exodus 14:1-31). This demonstration of awesome power led the Israelites to fear God and believe (trust) both in Him and in His servant Moses (Exodus 14:31). In this sense, the climactic miracle of the Red Sea crossing and the daily miracle of the guiding cloud ***baptized*** all of the Israelites ***into Moses*** (1 Corinthians 10:2)—that is, into his leadership.

The same spiritual food . . . drink (10:3-4). Likewise, all of the Israelites were fed for forty years

98

on the manna that appeared miraculously as a divine gift. It was physical food, but it was spiritual in that its origin was supernatural and divine, and in that it pointed beyond itself to the spiritual reality that God is His people's true food.

Likewise, all of Israel drank the physical water God provided supernaturally in the desert. The Old Testament tells of two occasions on which Moses got water from a *rock*, at the beginning and the end of the journey (Exodus 17:1-7, Numbers 20:2-13). Jewish legend said that this same rock followed the nation throughout the forty years. Paul does not endorse this legend, but he does say that Israel's true refreshment came not from the physical rock but from *the spiritual rock that accompanied them, and that rock was Christ.*

For a Jew to call Christ the Rock was quite a statement. The Old Testament repeatedly uses this metaphor for God (Deuteronomy 32:4,15,18,30-31; Psalm 18:2,31; 19:14; 28:1).

John Calvin and other commentators think that just as Paul refers to baptism in 1 Corinthians 10:2, he alludes to communion in 10:3-4.[1]

For Further Study:
a. Using a concordance, find references to manna throughout the Scriptures. What was it literally, and what did it represent spiritually? What New Testament truth did it foreshadow?

b. In John's Gospel, read about how Jesus is the true bread and the source of living water. What do these statements mean?

2. All of Israel (the word *all* occurs five times in 10:1-4) shared in the redemption from slavery, the baptism, and the spiritual food and drink. However, why didn't their "baptism" and "communion" guarantee that all escaped destruction (10:5-6)?

_____

_____

_____

_____

With most of them (10:5). The entire generation that was of military age died in the desert, except for Joshua and Caleb (Numbers 14:20-24,28-35; Deuteronomy 1:34-40).

99

For Further Study:
On Israel's grumbling,
see Numbers 11:1 or
16:41-50.

**Optional
Application:** Have
you been tempted to
participate in idolatry,
sexual immorality,
testing the Lord, or
grumbling? If so, what
should you do about
this?

Idolaters (10:7). When the Israelites felt that Moses
was too long in returning from Mount Sinai,
they persuaded Aaron to forge a golden calf for
them (Exodus 32:1-6). In worship to this fertil-
ity god, they feasted, got drunk, danced, and
debauched. This was the typical procedure in
idol feasts not only of Egypt and Canaan, but
also of Corinth in Paul's day.

Sexual immorality (10:8). At one point in their
journey, the Israelite men were enticed to join
the women of Moab in a feast before their gods.
The men attended both the sacrifices and the
feast, then participated in the orgy that followed
(Numbers 25:1-9). Likewise, the worship of
Corinth's most popular deity, Aphrodite, invari-
ably involved ritual prostitution, and other
feasts tended to degenerate into orgies.

Test the Lord (10:9). That is, "see how far his
patience will stretch or question if he means
what he says."[2] The Israelites tested God's faithfulness and patience by demanding regular food
and water instead of trusting God and accepting
the water (Numbers 21:5-9).

3. What evil actions cost many of the Israelites
their places among God's people (1 Corinthians
10:7-10)?

4. Why has God given us the stories of Israel's experiences (10:6,11)?

5. What can you learn from the case of Israel described in 10:1-10? How is it relevant to your life?

_____

_____

_____

_____

_____

6. What lesson does Paul draw from Israel's experience (10:12)?

_____

_____

_____

_____

7. Should this threat make you panic? (After all, so many Israelites fell to temptation!) Why or why not (10:13)?

_____

_____

_____

_____

_____

8. What steps does 10:13 imply you should take to resist temptation to sin?

_____

_____

_____

_____

_____

For Thought and Discussion: What does Paul mean by saying that "the fulfillment of the ages has come" upon us (10:11)?

For Thought and Discussion: Why is it significant that every temptation you encounter is "common to man" (10:13)?

Application to the topic of idol feasts
(10:14-22)

9. How does 10:1-13 apply to the topic Paul began in 8:1? (Consider 10:6-7,11-12 and the conclusion in 10:14.)

_____

_____

_____

_____

Cup of thanksgiving (10:16). This was the name of the third cup in the Passover feast. Jesus may have used this cup in instituting the Lord's Supper. It was a cup of thanksgiving in that a prayer of thanks to God was said over it: "Blessed art thou, O Lord our God, King of the universe, who createst the fruit of the vine."[3] The early Christians came to call the Lord's Supper "the Eucharist" from the Greek *eucharistos*, "thanksgiving." They, too, said a prayer of thanks over the cup.

Participation (10:16). *Koinonia* means "communion," "fellowship," "partnership," "sharing," "participation." (See the note on 1:9, page 23.) To receive the cup or the bread is to receive Christ, to have fellowship with Him in some way. The nature of that communion is debated, but the fact of it is not.

One loaf . . . one body (10:17). Of the bread Jesus said, "This is my body" (11:24). The Church is also His Body (12:12-26). The early Christians used one loaf to depict this oneness.

Demons (10:20). The Greek word *daemon* covered the range of spiritual entities from impersonal forces to personal beings, from weak imps to powerful demons. To the pagans, some *daemonae* were benevolent to humans, some were neutral, and some were malevolent. Most could be influenced or appealed to by magical and religious rites. From the Jewish and Christian perspective, any *daemon* that was not in submission to the Creator God (as angels are) was rebellious and wicked. Further, no *daemon* should be either worshiped or appealed to by magical or religious rituals.

Cup of demons (10:21). It was customary to pour out an offering of wine to the patron god of a feast to show that the whole feast was consecrated to that god.[4]

For Further Study:
Read the accounts of the Last Supper in Matthew 26:17-30, Mark 14:12-26, and Luke 22:14-23.

Optional Application: How do you think 1 Corinthians 10:16-22 should affect your attitude toward the Lord's Supper?

For Further Study:
On the Lord's jealousy (10:22), see Exodus 20:3-5, Deuteronomy 32:21, and Psalm 78:58. Why is it important for you to know that the Lord is a jealous God? Do you provoke Him to jealousy by any of your actions? If so, what should you do about this?

10. Since eating at the Lord's table is a participation in Christ (10:16), and since eating the Jew-

103

For Thought and Discussion: What if you were invited to a party that would include a sacrifice to a pagan god, a great deal of food and alcohol, ritual oaths to the god, and possibly sexual activity? Do you think it would be possible for you to attend such a party without dishonoring Christ? Why or why not?

For Thought and Discussion: Some of the "strong" believers in Corinth may have argued that matters of food and sex are religiously indifferent since they affect the body rather than the spirit. The "strong" may even have felt they could participate in rituals for nonexistent gods without offending Christ. How would Paul respond to these views (6:12-20; 10:12-13,18-22)?

ish sacrifices is a participation in the Jewish altar (10:18), what is the obvious conclusion about eating at a dinner party in a pagan temple (10:19-22)?

_____

_____

_____

_____

_____

Summary (10:23-11:1)

The same principle that applies to sex (6:12) applies to food and dinner parties (10:23).

11. What are Paul's conclusions about the following situations?

May a Christian buy meat in the market that may have been involved in a pagan ritual (10:25-26)? Why or why not?

_____

_____

_____

_____

_____

May a Christian attend a dinner party at the home of a pagan and eat whatever is served, even if it may have been a sacrifice (10:27)? Why or why not (8:4-6, 9:21-23, 10:30)?

_____

_____

_____

_____

_____

Should a Christian eat meat if someone at the dinner points out that it has been sacrificed (10:28-29)? Why or why not?

_____

_____

_____

_____

_____

Should a Christian attend a dinner in a pagan temple? Why or why not (10:11-23)?

_____

_____

_____

_____

12. What principles for making ethical decisions do you find in . . .

8:9,13; 10:32 _____

_____

_____

9:19-23 _____

_____

_____

9:24-27 _____

_____

_____

For Further Study:
a. When Paul says he tries to please everybody (10:23) and becomes all things to all men (9:22), why doesn't this contradict his teaching that "If I were still trying to please men, I would not be a servant of Christ" (Galatians 1:10)? Study the context of each statement. In what ways does Paul go out of his way to please people, and for what reasons? In what ways and for what reasons does he refuse to please people?
b. How do Paul's principles apply to your current situation? Is your present circumstance one in which you should bend to others' preferences for the sake of the gospel, or one in which for the sake of the gospel you should refuse to bend?

For Thought and Discussion: a. Discuss how 8:1–11:1 applies to your accepting or rejecting invitations to one or more of the following: a bar, a discothéque, a casino, a party at which alcohol is served, a party at which drugs are used, a nonChristian religious service, a séance, a martial arts session, a yoga class.

b. Would your answer be different if you were attending for evangelistic purposes? Why or why not? What principles should determine your decisions on such matters?

10:12 _____

_____

_____

10:13 _____

_____

_____

10:23 _____

_____

_____

10:24 _____

_____

_____

10:25-26 _____

_____

_____

_____

10:27-30 _____

_____

_____

_____

10:31 _____

_____

_____

10:33-11:1 _____

_____

_____

_____

Your response

For Further Study:
Add 8:1–11:1 to
your outline of
1 Corinthians.

13. What one truth or principle from 10:1–11:1
    would you like to apply to your own life?

_____

_____

_____

_____

14. How would you like this truth to affect your
    decisions, priorities, and attitudes?

_____

_____

_____

_____

15. What specific action do you think you should
    take in light of this truth?

_____

_____

_____

_____

_____

16. List any questions you have about 10:1–11:1.

_____

_____

_____

For the group

Warm-up. Ask everyone to think of a recent time
when he or she was invited to attend or participate
in some activity that was morally questionable. This

might be a social occasion with neighbors, a business function, etc. Ask anyone who can recall such a situation to tell briefly what the invitation was and what he or she decided to do.

Questions. There is a great deal of material in this chapter. You could easily spend two meetings on it. If you have only one meeting, try to draw out the key principles Paul gives in each paragraph for deciding what to participate in and what to avoid. What lessons can you draw from the example of Israel? From the comparison between the Lord's Supper and dinners in temples?

One of the "For Thought and Discussion" questions invites you to think of contemporary situations that might be comparable to the invitations to pagan homes and temples. Choose a few that are relevant to your group. For example, if you were engaged in sharing the gospel with the couple who live next door to you, would you attend a New Year's Eve party at their home that you suspected might include drunkenness and carousing? Would you be "all things to all men" (9:22) in this situation and rely on your ability to resist temptation? Or, would you "be careful that you don't fall" (10:12)? Would you be concerned that attending such a party would be a stumbling block to your fellow Christians?

Prayer. Thank God for the history of Israel that teaches you so many valuable lessons. Praise Him for punishing idolatry, immorality, testing, and grumbling. Thank Him for providing a way out of every temptation. Thank Him for the Lord's Supper, by which you participate in the body and blood of Christ. Praise Him that all food is clean because all the world belongs to Him. Ask Him to give you wisdom to decide what activities you should and shouldn't involve yourself in. Seek specific guidance regarding any decisions now facing members of your group.

1. Morris, page 142.
2. Bruce, *1 and 2 Corinthians*, page 92.
3. Bruce, *1 and 2 Corinthians*, page 94; see also Morris, page 145.
4. Bruce, *1 and 2 Corinthians*, page 97.

1 CORINTHIANS 11:2-34

Propriety in Worship

Pride was a pervasive problem in the church of Corinth. Some of the Corinthians boasted of the eloquence or wisdom of their favorite leaders. Some were arrogant about their liberation from old-fashioned morality. Others were proud of their ability to remain celibate. Still others were puffed up about their knowledge and freedom to eat anything and attend any pagan function without defilement or temptation. In the midst of all this, they could even write proudly to Paul that they were "remembering [him] in everything and holding to the teachings, just as [he] passed them on to [them]" (11:2)!

Paul never lost a chance to praise his readers for anything he honestly could, especially when he had to go on with more criticism. From 11:2 through 14:40, the issues all revolve around disorder in public worship, and the root of the disorders is consistently pride. As you read 11:2-34, look for signs of pride in the Corinthian church, and ask God to reveal any areas of pride in you.

Veiling women (11:2-16)

1. What unseemliness in public worship does Paul rebuke in 11:3-16?

_____

_____

_____

Head (11:3-10). It is generally agreed that the Greek and Jewish concepts of the head were not the same as ours. For example, they did not know modern neurophysiology and believed that a person thought with his midsection.[1] However, what they did believe about the head is debated:

1. Some say that the head primarily connotes honor—the head is the highest and most honorable part of the body; the feet are the lowest and least honorable (notice the references to honor in 11:4-5).[2]

2. Others point to references implying that the head suggests source or origin. The source of woman was originally man (Genesis 2:21-23, 1 Corinthians 11:8), the source of man is Christ, and the source of Christ is God (3:23, 8:6).[3]

3. Still others acknowledge the ideas of honor and source, but they feel that these imply authority. The one who is the source and is accorded prior honor has some kind of authority over the other (Ephesians 1:21-22, 5:22-23; Colossians 1:18, 2:10).[4]

With his head covered (11:4). Today it is a rule that Jewish men cover their heads in worship, but apparently it was not so in Paul's day. The Greek for "covered" implies something hanging down over the head like a veil, rather than a cap or hat.[5]

With her head uncovered (11:5). In Paul's day, proper women kept their hair long and went about in public with their heads veiled. Immoral women *cut* or *shaved* (11:6) their hair and went about with uncovered heads. Pagan prophetesses often prophesied with their heads uncovered and their hair disheveled to signify an ecstatic state.[6]

Image and glory (11:7). Both male and female are created in the image of God (Genesis 1:26-27). However, man was created to be the glory of God, while woman was made to be the glory of man. "Glory" means the expression of someone's nature and attributes.

Because of the angels (11:10). The angels were considered to be "guardians of the created order."

110

The Dead Sea Scrolls of a certain Jewish group mention the angels' presence at public worship. Hence, they were apparently interested in worship being done in a seemly manner.[7]

A sign of authority (11:10). Some interpreters think the veil is a sign that the woman is under the authority of her husband.

Others think it reflects the Near Eastern view of the veil: one may insult an unveiled woman in the street, but a veiled woman has dignity, security, and respect.

Still others think that a Christian woman's veil displays her authority in worship. A Jewish woman was irrelevant in the synagogue; her presence did not even help make up the required quorum of ten (there had to be ten males present for a service); she had to remain cloistered and silent. By contrast, in Christ the woman received equal status in worship; she could pray or prophesy alongside the men. Her veil signified her authority under God, just as a man's uncovered head signified his. However, because the created order (first man, then woman) has not been abolished, and its guardians (the angels) remain present, the woman's sign of authority is a veil, while a man's is an uncovered head.[8]

---

2. Why does it dishonor a man's head to pray or prophesy with his head covered (11:3-4,7,14)?

_____

_____

_____

3. Why does it dishonor a woman's head to pray or prophesy with her head uncovered (11:3,5-10,14-15)?

_____

_____

_____

For Further Study:
Using a concordance, research the use of the word *head* in the New Testament.

For Thought and Discussion: To understand 11:8-9, read Genesis 2:4-24.

4. What do you think Paul means by "head" in 11:3? Why? (Support your answer with Scripture.)

_____

_____

_____

_____

5. What does it mean that man is the image and glory of God (11:7)?

_____

_____

_____

_____

6. What does it mean that woman is the image of God but the glory of man?

_____

_____

_____

_____

7. How does 11:11-12 balance 11:7-9?

_____

_____

_____

_____

_____

8. Do you think women should cover their heads in public worship today? Why or why not?

_____

_____

_____

_____

9. What other principles and applications do you think 11:2-16 has for Christians today?

_____

_____

_____

_____

For Thought and Discussion: Do you think the common practice of churches should bind you and your church to conform (**11:16**)? Why or why not?

The Lord's Supper (11:17-34)

It is bad enough that the Corinthian believers are needlessly flouting social convention to assert their Christian liberty (11:3-16). Their behavior at the Lord's table is even worse.

Eat (11:20-22). The early Church held a full meal along with the Lord's Supper. It was called the *agape* ("love feast" in Jude 12). It was supposed to be like a potluck dinner, with each member bringing something to share. However, it seems that in Corinth, the rich were arriving early with the fine meats and wines they were used to, and going ahead without the rest. The poorer members (slaves and artisans, the "weak" we have already heard about in 1:26-28, 8:7-13) arrived later when they had gotten off work. They had to make do with the scanty food they were able to bring.

When pagan aristocrats gave feasts, it was customary for them to invite their entire households. The slaves and servants received smaller portions and cheaper wine than the higher class guests. Evidently, the rich members of the

113

church considered this appropriate in the Christian love feast as well.

New covenant (11:25). The old covenant (pact, treaty, agreement of relationship) between God and Israel was sealed with the blood of sacrificed animals (Exodus 24:3-8). After Israel sinned severely against that covenant, God promised that one day He would make a new covenant with His people, in which He would forgive their sins and write His Law on their hearts (Jeremiah 31:31-34). The shed blood of Jesus sealed and made possible the new covenant.

Recognizing the body of the Lord (11:29). "Judge the body rightly" in NASB. "Recognizing" is *diakrino*, "to discern," "to distinguish," or "to separate." The same verb is rendered in *if we judged ourselves* (11:31). That is, if we *examine* ourselves (11:28) and discern the body of the Lord in the communion service, we will discern what we are really like and not fall under the kind of judgment Paul refers to in 11:30.

To recognize the body of the Lord may mean to discern that the crucified body of the Lord is present in the communion meal. It may mean to distinguish the Lord's Supper from ordinary meals because the body of the Lord is present or is symbolized. Or it may mean to discern the oneness of the body of believers in this meal in which one loaf is used to represent that one body (10:17). All of these layers of meaning may be intended: the one loaf is the body of the Lord broken for His people to make them into one body.

10. What essential truths about the Lord's Supper and Jesus' work for us can you glean from 11:23-26?

_____

_____

_____

_____

_____

_____

_____

11. a. Why is the Lord's Supper an essential part of
       our task of spreading the gospel (11:26)?

       _____

       _____

       _____

       _____

**For Thought and
Discussion:** What do
you think should be
your attitude toward
the Lord's Supper?
Why?

**For Thought and
Discussion:** How
does eating and
drinking this meal
proclaim the Lord's
death until He comes
(11:26)?

    b. How should this fact affect the way we cele-
       brate it?

       _____

       _____

       _____

       _____

       _____

12. Why should we be careful to avoid taking the
    Lord's Supper in an unworthy manner
    (11:27,29-30)?

    _____

    _____

    _____

    _____

    _____

13. What does Paul mean by "an unworthy manner"?

    11:18-22 _____

    _____

    _____

    _____

For Thought and Discussion: How do you think you should go about examining yourself before participating in the Lord's Supper?

For Thought and Discussion: What does it tell you about communion that some in Corinth had actually sickened and even died because they did not take communion with the proper attitude (11:30)?

11:28-29,31 _____

_____

_____

_____

14. In 4:3-4, Paul says he does not judge himself but lets the Lord judge him. In 11:28-31, he says one should examine and judge (discern) himself so that he will not receive a disciplinary judgment.

    Study the context of each passage carefully. What kind of self-examination/discernment/judgment do you think Paul commends, and what kind does he rebuke?

commends _____

_____

_____

_____

_____

rebukes _____

_____

_____

_____

_____

Your response

15. What insight from 11:2-34 seems most relevant to your current life?

_____

_____

_____

_____

_____

16. How would you like this to affect your priorities and practices?

For Further Study: Add 11:2-34 to your outline.

_____

_____

_____

_____

_____

17. What steps can you take, with God's help, to begin letting this happen?

_____

_____

_____

_____

_____

18. List any questions you have about 11:2-34.

_____

_____

_____

_____

For the group

Warm-up. Ask one or two group members to describe what the Lord's Supper means to them personally. How important is it in your life, and why?

Read aloud. You may want to take this chapter in two sections, reading 11:2-16 before you discuss that passage, and 11:17-34 before you discuss it.

Questions. Both sections of this chapter are full of thorny issues for interpretation and application. What does Paul mean by "head"? Should women today cover their heads in church? What does "this

117

is my body" mean? What does it mean to recognize the body? How should we examine and judge ourselves, and how should we not? Try to maintain an atmosphere in which differing views are respected and no one feels contempt for another because of his interpretations. At the same time, try to wrestle with the text and come to personal convictions based on what it says, rather than what you might wish it says. Find some concrete ways of making these passages relevant to your lives. If you want to get through the whole chapter in one meeting, plan to divide your time evenly between the two sections. Don't let a debate about 11:2-16 keep you from discussing 11:17-34.

Wrap-up.

Prayer. Praise God for instituting the order in which He is head of Christ, Christ is head of man, and man is head of woman. Praise Him for the way He made man and woman to complement each other with their respective roles. Ask Him to help each of you understand and fulfill your own role in His Kingdom.

Thank Jesus for giving Himself up to betrayal and death for you. Thank Him for His body and His blood that inaugurated the new covenant. Ask Him to help each of you examine yourself and recognize His body in the Lord's Supper. Thank God for disciplining you so that you will not be condemned with the world.

If your group is interested, consider ending your meeting with a simple communion service in which you actively proclaim the Lord's death.

1. Morris, page 152.
2. *The NIV Study Bible*, page 1748.
3. Bruce, *1 and 2 Corinthians*, page 103.
4. Morris, pages 151-152.
5. Bruce, *1 and 2 Corinthians*, page 104.
6. Morris, page 152; Bruce, *1 and 2 Corinthians*, pages 104-105.
7. Bruce, *1 and 2 Corinthians*, page 106.
8. Bruce, *1 and 2 Corinthians*, page 106.

LESSON THIRTEEN

1 CORINTHIANS 12:1-31

Spiritual Gifts: 1

Pride, arrogance, being "puffed up." Divisions, differences, factions. Over and over, the former have led to the latter in the Corinthian church. We've seen factions over leaders, discord over personal and business ethics, conflict over sacrificial meat, disorder over veiling women, and divisions between rich and poor at the Lord's table itself. Now Paul comes to another question the Corinthians wrote to him about: What are his views on spiritual gifts? And once again, prideful divisions are at the root of the problem. It seems that some members of the Corinthian church are proud of the spectacular gifts they possess and are looking down on those who lack those gifts. It takes Paul three chapters to set his readers straight on this matter, but in the process, he strikes the core of what the Corinthians need to understand.

As you read 12:1-31, ask the Lord to illuminate to you the essence of what He desires His Church to be.

Spiritual gifts (12:1-11)

Spiritual gifts (12:1). Literally, "spirituals." Paul could mean spiritual gifts or the people who possess them. We've seen this word (*pneumatikon*, a form of *pneumatikos*) before in 2:12-3:4, when Paul was rebuking the Corinthians for boasting about leaders. The word for

119

For Further Study:
Compare Paul's words
about being spiritual
in 2:12–3:4 to what
he says about this in
12:1–14:40. Evaluate
yourself by these
standards.

a spiritual gift Paul uses most often is *cha-risma. Pneumatikon* emphasizes that the gift is from the Spirit (*pneuma*), and *charisma* stresses that it is a gift (*charis* means "grace").

"It was universally accepted in antiquity that some people, who were in specially close touch with the divine, had special spiritual endowments. Usually this was understood in terms of trances, ecstatic speech, and the like. From the day of Pentecost on, there were some within the Christian Church who manifested such spiritual gifts. While the Holy Spirit was given to all believers [Romans 8:9,14], yet He came to some in a special way, so that they did unusual things such as speaking in a tongue they did not understand. To many early believers this kind of thing was pre-eminently the hallmark of a 'spiritual' man. By comparison the practice of Christian virtue seemed staid and colourless. Paul's discussion of this subject is epoch-making. . . . It is clear that he assigns to the so-called 'spiritual' gifts no such place of eminence as they were accorded in popular esteem."[1]

Mute idols (12:2). Those who are proud should remember who used to lead them astray. However mute the idols were, though, it was well known that the gods (or demons, 10:20) spoke through them and human intermediaries. The oracles of Apollo (such as the one at Delphi) were famous. Prophecy and ecstatic speech in unknown languages were reasonably common (see Acts 16:16). Such spectacular gifts, and the demons who inspired them, **led astray** most of the inhabitants of the known world.

Since Christians did not have a corner on the gift market, and since people were so easily led astray by the counterfeits, Paul gave a test for discerning true gifts from false ones in 12:3.

Lord (12:3). The Greek Old Testament used this word to translate the Hebrew name of God, *YHWH* (the LORD in NIV). Any Jew knew that "Jesus is Lord" implied "Jesus is God." Loyal citizens swore an oath, "Caesar is Lord," when taking political office. Thus, "Jesus is Lord," the great confession of the early Church, led to intense strife with both Jews and Romans.

1. Obviously, one can *say* "Jesus is Lord" without being inspired by the Holy Spirit. What do you think Paul means in 12:3?

For Further Study: Compare the test in 1 Corinthians 12:3 to the one in 1 John 4:1-3.

_____

_____

_____

_____

_____

Spirit . . . Lord . . . God (12:4-6). All *gifts, service,* and *working* are from the one Triune God, who Himself is Trinity in Unity.

---

2. For what purpose are spiritual gifts given (12:7)? Explain in your own words.

_____

_____

_____

_____

3. What are some of the implications of this fact for your life?

_____

_____

_____

_____

Wisdom (12:8). "The highest mental excellence"[2]— a grasp of the way the world works and the ability to apply this grasp in life.

Knowledge (12:8). Since Paul associates this with mysteries, revelation, and prophecy (13:2, 14:6),

121

he may be thinking of supernatural knowledge, "a meaning which is common in Hellenistic Greek."[3] He may also be implying that all accurate knowledge a Christian possesses is a gift of the Spirit.

Faith (12:9). All believers are gifted with saving faith in the Lord, but some are endowed with faith for special service (13:2).

Gifts of healing (12:9). Literally, "gifts of healings." These are various endowments to heal various kinds of disease and sickness. (See the book of Acts.)

Miraculous powers (12:10). Mighty works other than healings. Jesus, for instance, stilled a storm and fed multitudes with a small amount of food. Paul blinded a magician (Acts 13:11). Ananias and Sapphira were struck dead after Peter pronounced their guilt (Acts 5:1-11). Exorcisms might come under this category. In the Gospels and Acts, miraculous works are meant as signs of God's Kingdom and evidence of His power and will.

Prophecy (12:10). Speech inspired by the Holy Spirit for some purpose of God. This includes predictions of the future (Acts 11:28, 21:10-11) and instruction, commendation, and rebuke in the present (Acts 13:1-2, 1 Corinthians 14:29-30). A person might have this gift only occasionally (Acts 19:6) or as a permanent office (1 Corinthians 12:28-29).

Distinguishing between spirits (12:10). Every Christian needs this in some degree (1 John 4:1). It is the ability to tell whether a prophecy or miracle or teaching or counsel comes from the Holy Spirit or an unholy spirit. It is also the ability to discern if a person is afflicted by an evil spirit.

Tongues (12:10). Speech in a language that the speaker does not know. This may be a human language unknown to the speaker or a non-human language that can be understood only by someone divinely gifted with **the interpretation of tongues**.

4. What is Paul's point in 12:8-11?

_____

_____

_____

_____

_____

The body (12:12-31)

5. How are Christian believers like a human body (12:12-13)?

_____

_____

_____

_____

_____

For Further Study: On 12:13, see Matthew 3:11, John 3:3-5, Romans 8:15-17.

For Thought and Discussion: Does 12:13 suggest that there are any believers who haven't been baptized by or in the Spirit? Explain.

By one Spirit (12:13). The word *by* (Greek: *en*) does not mean that the Spirit does the baptizing. Rather, it means "in." Paul likens the Spirit to a fluid in which we are immersed. Later in this verse, he compares the Spirit to a fluid that fills us. (The verb "drink" is used of watering plants and irrigating fields as well as of giving people drink.)[4]

6. Paul defines the baptism of the Holy Spirit in 12:13. What do you think the following statements mean?

"we were all baptized by one Spirit into one body"

_____

_____

123

Optional Application: a. How well is the Body functioning in your life? Are you aware of needing and being needed by the Christians around you? Are you honoring the contributions of others? Do you suffer with those who suffer and rejoice with those who are honored?

b. Pray and examine your life. How do you need to grow in this area? Ask God to make you more aware of belonging to the Body, of having both needs and responsibilities.

_____

_____

_____

"we were all given the one Spirit to drink"

_____

_____

_____

_____

_____

7. The Latin word for "body," *corpus*, gives us the word *corporate*, "as a body." What are the implications of our corporateness for . . .

Christians who feel inferior to other Christians (12:14-20)?

_____

_____

_____

_____

_____

Christians who feel superior to other Christians (12:21-24)?

_____

_____

_____

_____

_____

all of us (12:25-26)? _____

_____

_____

_____

_____

_____ ___

Optional Application: Do you think of the weaker members of your church or fellowship as indispensable (**12:22**)? How should this affect the way you treat them and make decisions?

8. Why is 12:18 important to you?

_____

_____

_____

_____

_____

9. Paul says it is good for the Corinthians to "eagerly desire the greater gifts" (12:31). What are these greater gifts? (Consider 12:8-11,28-30; 14:1.)

_____

_____

_____

_____

Your response

10. What one truth from chapter 12 would you like to take to heart this week?

_____

_____

_____

_____

_____

11. How have you already seen this truth affecting your life?

_____

_____

_____

_____

_____

12. How would you like it to affect your actions and attitudes more deeply?

_____

_____

_____

_____

_____

13. What steps can you take to put this into practice, with God's help?

_____

_____

_____

_____

_____

14. List any questions you have about 12:1-31.

_____

_____

_____

_____

For the group

Warm-up. Ask, "If you had to compare your function in the Body of Christ to some part of a human body, how would you respond? A hand? An eye? A brain cell? A liver? Why?" Your group may have some creative (perhaps funny) ideas and a strong sense of what each person's contribution is. Or, group members may feel they have no idea what they contribute to the Body. Their answers to this question will show you how hard the idea of really belonging to the Body is for their hearts to grasp.

Questions. Corporateness is an extremely difficult concept for modern Americans with our tradition of rugged individualism. It is common for people to attend church and worship privately without becoming deeply involved in the lives of other believers. Your small group should be a place to practice being *members* (limbs, organs, parts) of the Body. But group members' feelings about themselves and each other may get in the way. For example, some may feel they have little of value to contribute to the Body, while others may be self-reliant through years of having no one they felt they could trust. If answers to questions lead you to think this is true of your group, take time to discuss the issue of relying on and being available for each other. How can you act as the Body in your group, suffering and rejoicing with each other, valuing and contributing to each other?

Discussing how you can be the Body more fully is probably more fruitful than debating whether or not gifts like tongues, miracles, and prophecy are used today. If this is a serious point of contention in your group, ask a couple of people to take about five minutes each to present the scriptural rationale for each view. If necessary, agree to disagree, but don't get bogged down in this issue.

Prayer. After a discussion about being the Body is an excellent time to pray for each member's needs specifically. Encourage each person to be open about his or her concerns and thanksgivings. Ask the Lord to help each of you trust, value, and care for the rest. Ask Him to reveal to each of you what your gifts for the common good of the Body are. Ask Him to show each of you how you can serve the rest. Ask Him to equip you with all you need to fulfill the jobs He has given you. Thank Him for drawing you together, for baptizing each of you by His Spirit into the Body, and for giving each of you that Spirit to drink.

1. Morris, page 165.
2. Morris, page 171.
3. Morris, page 171.
4. Morris, page 174; Bruce, *1 and 2 Corinthians*, pages 120-121.

1 CORINTHIANS 13:1-14:40

Spiritual Gifts: 2

It is good for the Corinthians to desire the greater spiritual gifts, but merely having great gifts is not the most excellent way to be a spiritual person (12:31). There are two truths one must grasp before he really understands the gifts. The first is that they are given for the common good of the Body (12:7-30). The second follows from the first (13:1-13).

In 13:1-14:40, read about the most excellent way to use God's gifts, asking God to show you how to put this into practice.

Love (13:1-13)

Love (13:1). The Greek word *agape* was not in common use before Christians chose it to express the characteristically Christian virtue. More common were words that mean fondness among friends and relatives (*philia*), affection between parent and child (*storge*), or passion between lovers (*eros*). But *agape* was the word Greek-speaking Jews used to express the love between God and His covenant people.[1]

"In secular Greek it represented a love in which the mind analyzes and the will chooses the object to be loved. Thus it is not a term wholly given to emotion, but it involves the whole man, emotions, intellect, and will. [*Agape*] is a deliberate, free act that is the

For Further Study:
a. Compare different translations of 13:4-7 to learn more about the meaning of love.
   b. Look up each of the descriptions of love in an English dictionary to explore their meanings.
   c. Search one of the Gospels to find examples of Jesus exemplifying each of these aspects of love.

decision of the subject rather than the result of unbidden, overpowering emotion."[2] Its greatest expression is the Father's love in giving up His Son for us, and the Son's love in giving up His own divine privileges, His purity from human sin, and His life (John 15:12-13; 2 Corinthians 5:21; Philippians 2:5-8; 1 John 3:16, 4:10).

1. Why are tongues, prophecy, faith, generosity, and even martyrdom worthless without love (13:1-3)? (Recall 8:1, 12:7.)

_____

_____

_____

_____

Patient (13:4). The word implies patience with people rather than with circumstances. The patient person does not retaliate when wronged.

2. Give examples of times when you have been called upon to show at least three of the aspects of love Paul names in 13:4-7.

a. _____

_____

_____

_____

_____

b. _____

_____

_____

_____

_____

130

c. _____

_____

_____

_____

_____

3. Which of the aspects of love in 13:4-7 do you find hardest to practice consistently, and why?

_____

_____

_____

_____

_____

When perfection comes (13:10). The Greek for "perfection" can mean "end," "fulfillment," "completeness," or "maturity." Paul is contrasting the partial and the complete. Some interpreters think the phrase refers to Christ's return. Others think it means the death of the Christian. Others understand it as the maturity or establishment of the Church, and others as the completion of the New Testament canon.[3]

4. Why is love more excellent than even the gifts listed in 12:28 (13:1-3,8-13)?

_____

_____

_____

_____

_____

For Thought and Discussion: How is it possible to acquire love as a habit (Romans 8:5-14, Galatians 5:23)?

For Thought and Discussion: a. Why won't prophecy, knowledge, and tongues be necessary in Heaven or when Jesus returns to bring the Kingdom in its fullness (13:8-12)?
b. Why will faith, hope, and love remain (13:13)?

For Thought and Discussion: What will we "see face to face" and "know fully" (13:12) "when perfection comes" (13:10)? What do you think Paul means by "when perfection comes"?

For Thought and
Discussion: Does
14:4,18-19 mean that
an interpretation for a
tongue is necessary
only in church but not
in private devotions?
Why or why not?

For Thought and
Discussion: How
does the quotation in
14:21 prove that
tongues are a sign for
unbelievers?

Prophecy and tongues (14:1-40)

5. What are the basic principles that should guide
   all use of spiritual gifts in worship services?

   14:12,26 _____

   _____

   _____

   14:20 _____

   _____

   _____

   14:33,40 _____

   _____

   _____

   _____

6. What does 14:20 mean? Explain in your own
   words.

   _____

   _____

   _____

   _____

   _____

7. These principles determine Paul's attitude
   toward the use of gifts like prophecy and
   tongues in the worship service. What does Paul
   say concerning each of these gifts?

   a. prophecy (14:1,39) _____

   _____

   (14:3-5) _____

   _____

   _____

   _____

132

(14:19) _____

_____

_____

(14:22,24-25) _____

_____

_____

_____

(14:29-33) _____

_____

_____

_____

b. tongues (14:2) _____

_____

_____

(14:4) _____

(14:5-12) _____

_____

_____

_____

(14:13) _____

_____

(14:14-17) _____

_____

_____

_____

(14:18) _____

_____

For Thought and Discussion: What is wrong with letting everyone in the worship service speak aloud in tongues at once (**14:23,27-28**)?

Optional Application: a. Does your church practice **14:27-28**? Should it? Why or why not?
b. Does your church practice **14:29-31**? Should it?

For Thought and Discussion: What scriptural and other evidence is there that 14:27-31 applies literally today, and what evidence is there that these verses applied literally only in the apostolic age?

(14:19) _____

_____

(14:21-23) _____

_____

_____

(14:27-28) _____

_____

_____

_____

(14:39) _____

8. How would you summarize Paul's attitude toward prophecy and tongues?

_____

_____

_____

_____

9. How is all this about prophecy and tongues relevant to you and your church or fellowship?

_____

_____

_____

_____

_____

_____

Women in church (14:33-40)

Silent (14:34). There are several main interpretations of this command:

134

1. God has ordained a timeless order in creation by which women must be in submission to their husbands both at home and in church (1 Corinthians 11:3, 14:34; Ephesians 5:22; 1 Timothy 2:11-12). Therefore, women should not be permitted to speak in church, regardless of the culture in which the church exists.

2. The order of creation is timeless, but how it applies to women speaking in church is not. Paul is concerned that the church be strengthened by believers showing respect for each other and for God in their use of spiritual gifts (14:26,30-31,33). Therefore, in a culture in which it is disgraceful for a woman to speak in church, she should remain silent out of respect and submission to the greater good. It was disgraceful in Paul's day for women to speak in religious services of both Jews and Gentiles (14:35). However, there were occasions when it was not disgraceful; a woman was free to pray or prophesy (11:5). Thus, Paul forbids women to speak only in cases when the social order regards it as disgraceful. An example in Paul's day might be women sitting in the service discussing the merits of a prophesy just given. The church has no business flouting social customs that do not conflict with the gospel.

3. In context, Paul is referring to women disrupting the worship service with noisy questions about tongues and prophecies (or other issues). Instead of clamoring for explanations right there, they should ask their husbands at home (14:35). Women are free to speak in proper ways (such as prayer and prophecy, 11:5), but they are not to interrupt. It was a new thing in Paul's day for women to be allowed to participate in public services, and many women had not been taught how to behave properly.[4]

---

10. What reasons does Paul give for saying that "women should remain silent in the churches" (14:32-40)?

For Further Study:
Add 12:1–14:40 to
your outline.

_____

_____

_____

_____

11. In light of 11:3,5; 14:33-40, what do you think Paul means by instructing women to remain silent in church?

_____

_____

_____

_____

_____

12. How is this relevant to your church?

_____

_____

_____

_____

_____

_____

Your response

13. What one aspect of 13:1-14:40 would you like to concentrate on for application this week?

_____

_____

_____

_____

_____

14. How would you like to grow in this area?

_____

_____

_____

_____

_____

15. What steps can you take to put this into practice?

_____

_____

_____

_____

_____

16. List any questions you have about 13:1-14:40.

_____

_____

_____

_____

For the group

Warm-up. Ask everyone to think of a time when they have experienced love during the past week. Let a few people describe their experiences briefly. It can be illuminating to look at concrete examples of love, rather than thinking of it in the abstract. If almost no one can recall being loved for the past week, plan to pray about the reasons for this at the end of your meeting. Are you aware of the love you are given?

Questions. You may find it most fruitful to concentrate on chapter 13. Look for practical ways each of you can grow in love.

There is a potential for argument on either the place of prophecy and tongues in church today or whether women should be silent in church. If the discussion starts to degenerate into opinions, remind the group that interpretations need to have scriptural support. Ask everyone to cite passages to back up their views. Cut the discussion short if it threatens to become an argument. Remind everyone what Paul has said about divisions and judging others for their views.

Prayer. Thank God for what He is teaching you. Praise Him as a God of order and peace. Ask Him to foster in each of you love that is patient, kind, humble, generous, and so on. Confess any ways in which you have failed to love others recently. Ask the Lord to teach you what gifts you should eagerly desire and how you should exercise them with love in an orderly manner for the building up of the Body.

1. Walther Günther and Hans-Georg Link, "Love," *The New International Dictionary of New Testament Theology,* volume 2, pages 538-547.
2. Donald W. Burdick, *The Letters of John the Apostle* (Chicago: Moody Press, 1985), page 140.
3. *The NIV Study Bible,* page 1752.
4. *The NIV Study Bible,* pages 1754-1755.

1 CORINTHIANS 15:1-34

Resurrection: 1

The last issue brought to Paul's attention is doctrinal. It is so central to the gospel and has such far-reaching implications for the Christian life that we can scarcely imagine the Corinthians arguing about it, but they were. Read 15:1-58 carefully, trying to follow the flow of Paul's reasoning on this subject.

1. Basically, what is chapter 15 about?

_____

_____

_____

2. What situation in Corinth seems to have prompted the need for this discourse (15:12)?

_____

_____

_____

Christ's resurrection (15:1-11)

3. In 15:3-8, Paul summarizes the essence of the gospel. What are its key points?

15:3 _____

15:4a _____

For Thought and Discussion: a. How can we avoid believing the gospel "in vain" (15:1-2)? How, in practice, does a person "hold firmly to the word I preached to you"?

b. What does this entail for you this week?

For Further Study: Paul says that Christ died for our sins and was raised "according to the Scriptures" (15:3-4). What Old Testament testimony is there that the Christ would die and be raised? See, for example, Psalm 16:8-11 and Isaiah 53:5-6,11-12.

139

For Further Study:
Read in Acts
7:57–8:3, 9:1-8 how
Paul persecuted the
church of God, and
how later the Lord
appeared to him.

**For Thought and
Discussion:** Why
does Paul stress that
all the apostles, not
just Paul himself,
preach the death and
resurrection of Christ
(15:11)? Consider
1:11-12.

**Optional
Application:** a. In
what ways is 15:10
true of you? What has
God's grace accom-
plished in you? What
is it even now
accomplishing?

b. Are there any
areas in which you
are resisting or not
trusting God's grace
to act in you? If so,
ask God to help you
trust Him and to act
through you as He has
chosen to do
(12:7,18). Then, act
in faith that He will
answer this prayer.

15:4b _____

15:5-8 _____

_____

_____

4. In this summary, what two kinds of evidence
does Paul give that Christ was indeed raised
from the dead?

_____

_____

_____

_____

_____

5. Listing Christ's resurrection appearances leads
Paul to reemphasize his apostolic authority
(which was being undermined in Corinth). In
what ways does Paul's apostleship rest solely on
God's grace?

15:9 _____

_____

15:10 _____

_____

The believer's resurrection (15:12-34)

Because most people of Paul's day believed that
matter was base while the soul or spirit was divine,
it was common to believe that the soul was immortal, but rare to believe in bodily resurrection. In
fact, many pagans found the idea that the corrupt
physical body would be raised to eternal life disgust-
ing. They thought of the body as the soul's prison,
and they wanted to be free of it. The idea of bodily
resurrection caused the sophisticates of Athens to
sneer at Paul (Acts 17:32).

Some pagans who converted to Christianity
just couldn't shake the idea that the body was

somehow inferior and corrupt. So, they concluded that the resurrection was merely spiritual: one dies and is raised spiritually with Christ in baptism. Eternal life meant eternal life of the soul. Paul himself taught the doctrine of spiritual death and resurrection in baptism (Romans 6:1-10), but he also insisted on a physical resurrection when Christ returns. The idea that bodies are essentially debased and so physical resurrection is impossible is contrary both to Old Testament views of the body and to the gospel of Christ.

For Further Study: Research what the Old Testament teaches about body, soul, and spirit. Is the body inferior to the soul?

For Thought and Discussion: Who are "those . . . who have fallen asleep in Christ" (15:18)?

6. How is the gospel of Christ's death and resurrection relevant to the dispute in Corinth (15:12-13)?

_____

_____

_____

_____

_____

7. If Christ has not in fact been raised, what is true of Christianity and Christians?

15:14 _____

_____

15:15 _____

_____

15:17 _____

_____

15:18 _____

_____

15:19 _____

_____

8. Why is our faith in Christ useless and pitiable if He has not been raised? What did His resurrection prove and accomplish?

Acts 17:31 _____

_____

_____

Romans 1:3-4 _____

_____

_____

Romans 4:25 _____

_____

_____

Romans 6:4,8-11 _____

_____

_____

_____

Romans 8:11 _____

_____

_____

Still in your sins (15:17). The Jewish Law stated that to be executed and hung on a tree was a sign that the person was accursed by God (Deuteronomy 21:23). The Jews concluded that anyone executed by crucifixion fell into this category. That may have been one of the reasons why the Jewish leaders insisted that Jesus be crucified rather than executed in some other way (John 19:6). Jesus died as a criminal in a manner that proved He was accursed. To the Jews, this proved He was not the Messiah. Clearly, a man under God's judgment could not justify others from their sins.

The apostles said the Resurrection proved Jesus had God's blessing, not His curse (Acts 2:24-36, 5:30-32, 13:32-39). Crucifixion was a sign of the curse on Jesus (Galatians 2:13-14), but resurrection showed that the curse was lifted.

Firstfruits (15:20). Each year, the Jews gave the first sheaf of the harvest to the Lord as a sign that the whole harvest belonged to Him (Leviticus 23:10-11,17,20).

Death came through a man (15:21). Adam's one act of disobedience brought a sinful nature and death to all his descendants (Genesis 2:17, 3:17-19; Romans 5:12-21). To be *in Adam* (15:22) is to be in union, fellowship, and solidarity with him—a member, as it were, of the body of Adam. "Adam" means "mankind" in Hebrew, and Adam is both the corporate personality of mankind and the individual who headed the race and gave it its characteristics. (Corporate personality is a typically Hebrew concept. Old Testament writers use "Israel" interchangeably to refer to an individual man and the nation that descended from him.)

Solidarity with Adam brings disaster on all those born into the family. However, the same principle of solidarity brings blessing on those who are reborn *in Christ*—into union and fellowship with Him.

Dominion, authority and power (15:24). All governing powers (human, spiritual) of any kind will be nullified.

The Son himself will be made subject (15:28). In function in the Kingdom, not in essential nature. The New Testament as a whole teaches that Father, Son, and Spirit are equal in deity and honor. Christ voluntarily and temporarily gave up His divine rights to become human for our sakes (Philippians 2:5-11), so in relation to the Kingdom He is subordinate to the Father.

9. Since Christ has been raised, what can we confidently expect? (Explain in your own words.)

15:20-23 _____

_____

_____

For Thought and Discussion: What does it mean that Christ is "the firstfruits of those who have fallen asleep" (15:20)?

For Thought and Discussion: Why is it important that Jesus was fully human as well as fully divine (15:21)?

For Further Study: Study the relationship between the Father, the Son, and the Spirit in the New Testament. Start with John's Gospel, then look at Romans 8:9-11, Hebrews 1:1-14, and other passages.

143

For Thought and Discussion: How is the quotation in 15:33 relevant to the debate about resurrection? Who is the "bad company" in the Corinthian church? Why are their beliefs, and the practices that arise from those beliefs, corrupting?

Optional Application: How can you imitate Paul's attitude in light of your confident expectation of resurrection? How can you offer yourself to die every day (15:30-31)? How can you risk life and comfort for the gospel?

15:24-28 _____

_____

_____

_____

_____

Baptized for the dead (15:29). This is a notoriously difficult phrase. The most natural meaning is that some members of the church at Corinth were being baptized on behalf of persons who had died. Since the second century AD, this has been declared a heretical practice, but it was known in the second century (and possibly in the first). Paul does not condemn the practice, but he speaks of **those**, not "we," who do it. He does not countenance it. It may be that an epidemic or something similar had taken the lives of a number of believers before they had a chance to be baptized. The Corinthians may then have been baptized for dead believers. It is hard to imagine Paul even tolerating baptism for people who had not even professed faith in Christ before their deaths.

Several dozen other explanations have been suggested. For example, Christians may have been baptized (1) in anticipation of the resurrection from the dead; (2) to fill the ranks of Christians who had died; or (3) in order to be reunited at the resurrection with those who had died.

10. What would Paul do differently if he stopped expecting resurrection (15:30-32)?

_____

_____

_____

_____

_____

11. Why is it a sin, and evidence of being ignorant of God, to deny the resurrection (15:34)?

_____

_____

_____

_____

_____

12. How would you summarize what Paul has said so far in chapter 15?

_____

_____

_____

_____

_____

Optional Application: How is it personally significant to you that ultimately death will be destroyed (15:26)?

Optional Application: If all powers in the world will ultimately be put under Jesus Christ (15:24), how should this affect the way you treat Jesus and the earthly powers now? How does this apply to specific situations you are facing?

Your response

13. What one truth from 15:1-34 would you like to take to heart this week?

_____

_____

_____

_____

14. How would you like this to affect your attitudes, priorities, and actions?

_____

_____

_____

_____

15. What steps can you take to begin putting this into practice, with God's help?

_____

_____

_____

_____

_____

16. List any questions you have about 15:1-34.

_____

_____

_____

For the group

Warm-up. Ask, "Does believing in resurrection affect your daily life? If so, how?" Hopefully, by the time you have discussed lessons fifteen and sixteen, the hope of resurrection will have begun to affect your lives in many and deep ways.

Questions. Don't get bogged down in speculating about baptism for the dead. This question will probably never be solved. Instead, explore the importance of Christ's resurrection and your future resurrection. How should these truths affect the way each of you leads your life?

Prayer. Thank God for the death, burial, resurrection, and appearances of Christ. Thank Him for what these have accomplished in your lives: the removal of sin, the hope of your own resurrection, and the meaning this gives to your life on earth now. Praise Him that the Kingdom will be fulfilled and handed over to the Father, and that all current powers will be rendered null. Ask the Lord to impress the hope of resurrection firmly on your hearts, so that you will risk your lives and comforts for the sake of the gospel. Pray for each member of your group to fully grasp the implications of this hope.

LESSON SIXTEEN

1 CORINTHIANS 15:35-58

Resurrection: 2

Paul has given a strong argument that Christians
will be raised from the dead when Christ returns:
We know bodily resurrection is possible because
Jesus was raised. Hundreds of people saw Him. And
if He wasn't raised, then He wasn't Christ, and our
sins are not forgiven. Furthermore, if we will not be
raised, then there is no point in risking our lives
and limiting our pleasures for the gospel; we might
as well indulge ourselves like pagans.

Okay, the Corinthians might answer. We see
that the whole gospel—the Christian hope of salvation, eternal life, and the Kingdom of God—rests on
the resurrection of Christ and His people. But that
doesn't get us past the problem that physical matter
just seems incompatible with eternal life. How can
bodies that age and decay exist in the Kingdom of
God? Surely what we are really talking about is an
immortal soul, aren't we?

For Paul's reply, read 15:35-58.

The resurrection body (15:35-49)

The Jewish idea of resurrection current in Paul's day
was that the raised body would be physically identical with the one that died. This seemed absurd to
those who saw that bodies decay into nothing.
"How are the dead raised?" (15:35) questions the
mechanism that could make this possible. "With
what kind of body will they come?" ridicules the
idea that a body could be raised identical to the

147

corpse that was buried. Paul recognizes that such questions are "foolish" (15:36).

1. How does Paul refute the objection that a resurrected, eternal body is hard to conceive of (15:35-49)?

15:36-38 _____

_____

_____

_____

15:39-41 _____

_____

_____

_____

15:42-43 _____

_____

_____

_____

15:45-49 _____

_____

_____

_____

Spiritual body (15:44). The **natural body** is *psychikon*, "soulish," suited to the earthly life animated by the natural soul. Adam, and all his descendants, were created as "a living soul" (Genesis 2:7, NASB margin; 1 Corinthians 15:45, NASB—the Greek is *psyche*). Christ, **the last Adam** (15:45) is **a life-giving spirit** able to impart the life of the Spirit to those who are "in

Christ." Those who are thus filled with the Holy Spirit are *pneumatikon*, "spiritual," in this life (1:12-16). But at the resurrection, they will take on bodies suited to this spiritual life: bodies able to express their spirits fully and fully animated by the Spirit in them. A spiritual body is not made of spirit, but expresses and is animated by the Spirit.

For Further Study: What can we learn about the nature of resurrected bodies from Jesus' resurrected body (Luke 24:13-42, John 20:10–21:14)?

2. Paul does not fully satisfy our curiosity about resurrected bodies. Still, we do know something about what we will be like (15:42-50). Paul explains by contrasting the first and last Adams. Fill in the chart below to describe the bodies of those who descend from the first and last Adams:

For Thought and Discussion: Does Paul teach that our bodies will be raised identical to the way they are buried? Explain.

first Adam	last Adam (Christ)
perishable	
dishonored	
weak	
natural (animated by and suited to the soul)	

149

For Thought and Discussion: Are you one of those "who are of heaven" (15:48)? What does this mean? How should it affect your life?

first Adam	last Adam (Christ)
a living soul	
made of dust of the earth	
origin in the earth	

3. Paul contrasts "those who are of the earth" with "those who are of heaven" (15:48). What does it mean to be "of heaven" rather than "of the earth"? What does this imply about these people other than the nature of their bodies?

_____

_____

_____

_____

Victory over death (15:50-58)

4. What do you think "We will not all sleep, but we will all be changed" (15:51) means?

_____

_____

_____

_____

150

5. Why must all natural, physical bodies be changed, even those that have not died (15:42-44,50,53)?

_____

_____

_____

_____

_____

_____

6. What will be the result when this occurs (15:54-55)?

_____

_____

_____

_____

7. Why is sin the sting of death (15:56)? (See, for instance, Romans 5:12, 6:23.)

_____

_____

_____

_____

8. How is the Law the power of sin (15:56)? (See Romans 4:15, 7:7-13.)

_____

_____

_____

_____

_____

For Further Study: Research the meaning of trumpets in Scripture. Why does a trumpet call herald the resurrection (15:52)? What do trumpets represent? (See, for example, Leviticus 25:9, Isaiah 27:13, Matthew 24:31, 1 Thessalonians 4:16-17, Revelation 11:15-18.)

Optional Application: a. How does 15:1-58 encourage you if you have lost a beloved believer to death?

b. How should this chapter affect your attitude toward your own future? What difference should it make to your life that death is defeated?

151

For Thought and Discussion: Does 15:54-57 mean Christians shouldn't grieve or hurt when loved ones die? Why or why not?

Optional Application: Are you afraid of dying? If so, tell God how you feel and ask Him for the grace to *know* that death has no sting for you. Memorize 15:54-55.

Optional Application: Specifically how can you put 15:58 into practice?

For Further Study: Add 15:1-58 to your outline.

9. Yet how has God given us the victory over sin, and therefore death, through Christ (15:57)? (*Optional:* See Romans 5:12-19; 6:6-7,14,22.)

_____

_____

_____

_____

_____

Your response

10. How do you think the truth that "Death has been swallowed up in victory" (15:54) should affect your life now?

_____

_____

_____

_____

11. Read 15:1-2,30-32,58. How does Paul say the fact of Christ's resurrection and the promise of your own should affect your attitudes and actions?

_____

_____

_____

_____

12. What truths in 15:35-58 would you especially like to take to heart?

_____

_____

_____

_____

13. What specific action (including prayer, memorizing a passage, and decisions about your current circumstances) would you like to take this week in response to these truths?

_____

_____

_____

_____

_____

_____

14. List any questions you have about 15:35-58.

_____

_____

_____

_____

For the group

Warm-up. Ask, "Try to remember your earliest encounter with death. Maybe a relative died when you were a child. How did the people around you act in that situation? How did you feel and act?" These early experiences can have a huge impact on our hearts even when we believe mentally that death has lost its sting for Christians.

Questions. To help us understand what a resurrected body will be like, Paul makes analogies to what we are familiar with. Just as a seed has one body, but after it "dies" and "is raised" it has another more glorious body, so will we. Just as bodies differ in the universe, so our bodies differ from the spiritual bodies we will have. But we will have bodies; we won't be disembodied spirits.

Once you understand what Paul teaches about resurrection, explore its implications for your lives. How can you live as those who are "of heaven," those who will one day bear the likeness of Christ?

153

What difference does it make to each of you that sin and death are defeated?

If you sense that some group member is still hurting over the loss of a loved one, plan to discuss this either as a group or privately with that person. It is normal to feel loss, sorrow, and even anger when a loved one dies, and some Christians feel guilty for not being content that their beloved is in heaven. It is not uncommon for people to feel the loss years later. You might want to gather one or two people to pray with a grieving group member.

Wrap-up.

Prayer. Thank God for the promise of glorious, imperishable, Spirit-enlivened, powerful bodies. Praise Him for defeating sin and death. Ask Him to enable you to live daily in the light of this precious hope.

1 CORINTHIANS 16:1-24 AND REVIEW

Personal Words

Paul has had some hard words for the Corinthians, but he closes with love and a confidence that they will remain as devoted to him as he to them. Observe the workings of the first century church as you read 16:1-24.

Requests and greetings (16:1-24)

For Further Study:
Read more about the collection for the poor in Jerusalem in Acts 20:1-6,16; 21:1-36; 24:17; Romans 15:23-33; and 2 Corinthians 8:1–9:14.

The collection for God's people (16:1). In answer to another question in the Corinthians' letter, Paul explains how he wants them to handle the collection for the poor believers in Jerusalem. When Paul was in Jerusalem several years earlier, the apostles had encouraged him to evangelize the Gentiles but had asked him to "continue to remember the poor" (Galatians 2:10). He had brought a contribution from the Gentile churches to the Jerusalem church during a famine, and the apostles wanted him to continue to do this. Jerusalem was a poor city; the Jews there were supported partly by contributions from Jews living abroad, but the Christians had no access to those funds.[1] They needed help from their spiritual offspring, and Paul was glad to aid them. He was taking up a collection among the churches he had planted as "(*a*) an acknowledgment by the Gentile churches of the spiritual debt they owed to the mother-church in Jerusalem, (*b*) a practical token to the Jerusa-

155

lem church of the genuineness of the Gentile Christians' faith, (c) a means of binding Jewish and Gentile Christians more closely together" (see Romans 15:25-28).[2]

Help me on my journey (16:6). Since there were no inns, restaurants, or grocery stores along the roads, it was customary for believers to house missionaries while they visited and supply them with food, drink, and equipment for their journeys.

Pentecost (16:8). The Greek name for the Feast of Weeks, the Jewish celebration of the wheat harvest (Leviticus 23:10-16). It was the fiftieth day after Passover (Pentecost means "fifty"), so it fell in late spring.

See . . . that he has nothing to fear (16:10). Timothy had a timid spirit (2 Timothy 1:7), and he was likely to be intimidated by the aggressive, proud Corinthians if they did not curb themselves.

Apollos (16:12). The Corinthians had evidently asked about him, and he apparently was or had been with Paul in Ephesus. Clearly, the divisions between the Paul and Apollos factions in Corinth did not reflect any ill feeling between the two men.

Aquila and Priscilla (16:19). This couple had helped Paul establish the church in Corinth and was now working with him in Ephesus.

Come, O Lord (16:22). The Aramaic expression *Maranatha* was so important to the faith of the early Christians that they took it over without translating it, just like *Amen, Hallelujah,* and *Hosanna.* The second coming of the Lord was a fervent hope.

---

1. What can we learn about the priorities, attitudes, lifestyle, and practices of the early Christians from 16:1-24? Write down everything you observe.

_____

_____

_____

_____

_____

_____

_____

_____

_____

Optional Application: Are there any attitudes, priorities, or practices in 16:1-24 that you think you should imitate? If so, what are they and how can you act on them?

Review

You began your study of 1 Corinthians with an overview, then spent several weeks examining passages in detail. Now it's time to take another overview to see how your perception of the book has changed and deepened. Some teachers call this the "spiral" approach to Bible study—you swing from broad view to narrow to broad, spiraling in on the message of the book. The better you grasp the overall message and intent of the book, the more accurate context you will have for interpreting and applying the details.

Begin your review by reading straight through 1 Corinthians at one sitting. You should be able to read quickly because the book should be familiar by now. Look for threads that tie the book together and for passages that shed light on other passages. Then look over your answers in lesson one and any outlining you have done.

2. What have you learned from 1 Corinthians about the following topics? (Choose at least six.)

   wisdom _____

   _____

   _____

   _____

_____

_____

_____

what it means to be "spiritual" _____

_____

_____

_____

_____

_____

divisions in the church _____

_____

_____

_____

_____

_____

judging _____

_____

_____

_____

_____

_____

_____

pride _____

_____

_____

_____

_____

_____

sexual morality _____

_____

_____

_____

_____

_____

marriage _____

_____

_____

_____

_____

_____

rights and freedoms _____

_____

_____

_____

_____

_____

_____

temptation to sin _____

_____

_____

_____

_____

the Lord's Supper _____

_____

_____

_____

_____

spiritual gifts _____

_____

_____

_____

_____

the Body of Christ _____

_____

_____

_____

love _____

_____

_____

_____

_____

_____

resurrection _____

_____

_____

_____

_____

_____

_____

3. In question 5 of lesson one (page 17), you said
   what you thought 1 Corinthians was basically
   about. After closer study, how would you now
   summarize why Paul wrote this letter and what
   it is about?

_____

_____

_____

_____

_____

4. How would you describe the Corinthians' biggest problem and its solution?

_____

_____

_____

_____

5. Review the questions you listed at the end of
   lessons one through sixteen. Do any remain
   unanswered? If so, record them again here.
   Some of the sources on pages 165-167 may
   help. Or, study some particular passage again
   with cross-references and commentaries, or ask
   some Christian whose scriptural background
   you trust.

_____

_____

_____

_____

_____

_____

6. Have you noticed any areas (thoughts, attitudes, opinions) in which you have changed as
   a result of studying 1 Corinthians? If so, how
   have you changed?

_____

_____

_____

_____

_____

7. Look back over the study at questions in which
   you expressed a desire to make some specific
   application. Are you satisfied with your follow-
   through? Pray about any of those areas, or any
   new areas, that you think you should continue
   to focus on. Write any plans for attention and
   action here.

_____

_____

_____

_____

_____

_____

_____

For the group

Warm-up. Ask, "In what ways are you involved with Christians in other countries?" One obvious undertone in chapter 16 is that the early churches were linked together, even though the distance between them was months of travel time rather than hours, as it is today. Paul expected the Corinthians to care about the believers in Jerusalem whom they had never seen. The Christians in Asia greeted their brethren in Corinth. Do the members of your group have similar attitudes, or do they feel isolated from believers in other countries?

Questions. Take five or ten minutes to let everyone share answers to question 1, then spend the bulk of your time on the review. Choose between two and six topics from question 2 that you think are most important for your group to discuss. Be sure to allow enough time for questions 3 through 7. If group members still have questions about the book, let other members answer them, or suggest some sources of answers.

Questions 6 and 7 allow you to evaluate how you have grown from studying and applying 1 Corinthians. This is not a time to feel guilty or self-satisfied, but a time to be encouraged, re-motivated, and enabled to keep going. If you don't see many results yet, ask yourselves whether you should act on or pray or think about application differently. But don't assume that you are doing something wrong. Transformation doesn't happen overnight. You may just need to persevere in your present approach to application and trust God for results.

Evaluation. Take a few minutes or a whole meeting to assess how your group functioned during your study of 1 Corinthians. Here are some questions to consider:

What did you learn about small group study?

How well did the study help you grasp 1 Corinthians?

What were the most important truths you discovered about the Lord?

What did you like best about your meetings?

What did you like least? What would you change?

163

How well did you meet the goals you set at your first meeting?

What are members' current needs? What will you do next?

Prayer. Thank God for all you've learned from studying 1 Corinthians together. Thank Him for the ways He has worked in each of your lives. Ask Him to show you what areas of your lives He wants to work on next, and ask Him to encourage each of you as He does so. Pray about any specific desires for application you dicussed during this meeting.

1. Morris, page 237.
2. Bruce, *1 and 2 Corinthians*, page 158.

STUDY AIDS

For further information on the material covered in this study, consider the following sources. If your local bookstore does not have them, ask the bookstore to order them from the publisher, or find them in a seminary library. Many university and public libraries also carry these books.

Commentaries on 1 Corinthians

You don't have to agree with everything in a commentary to find it helpful. Here are just a few of the many on 1 Corinthians.

Barrett, C. K. *First Epistle to the Corinthians* (Harper & Row, New Testament Commentaries, 1968).
> Written from a liberal point of view, but generally considered the most thorough and detailed scholarship on 1 Corinthians.

Bruce, F. F. *1 and 2 Corinthians* (Eerdmans, The New Century Bible Commentary, 1971).
> The comments are relatively brief (compared to Barrett's) but helpful, especially with historical background. Paperback.

Hodge, Charles. *1 Corinthians* (Nisbet, 1873).
> Many evangelicals consider Hodge's work a classic. It lacks much of the historical background of the newer works, but is full of examination of the text. Recent reprints may be available.

Morris, Leon. *The First Epistle of Paul to the Corinthians* (Eerdmans, Tyndale New Testament Commentaries, 1958).
> More thorough than Bruce and less than Barrett. A very readable and useful work for the beginning and experienced student alike. Paperback.

Histories, Concordances, Dictionaries, and Handbooks

A *history* or *survey* traces Israel's history from beginning to end, so that you can see where each biblical event fits. *A Survey of Israel's History* by Leon Wood (Zondervan, 1970) is a good basic introduction for laymen from a conservative viewpoint. Not critical or heavily learned, but not simplistic. Many other good histories are available.

A *concordance* lists words of the Bible alphabetically along with each verse in which the word appears. It lets you do your own word studies. An *exhaustive* concordance lists every word used in a given translation, while an *abridged* or *complete* concordance omits either some words, some occurrences of the word, or both.

The two best exhaustive concordances are *Strong's Exhaustive Concordance* and *Young's Analytical Concordance to the Bible*. Both are available based on the King James Version of the Bible and the New American Standard Bible. *Strong's* has an index by which you can find out which Greek or Hebrew word is used in a given English verse. *Young's* breaks up each English word it translates. However, neither concordance requires knowledge of the original language.

Among other good, less expensive concordances, *Cruden's Complete Concordance* is keyed to the King James and Revised Versions, and *The NIV Complete Concordance* is keyed to the New International Version. These include all references to every word included, but they omit "minor" words. They also lack indexes to the original languages.

A *Bible dictionary* or *Bible encyclopedia* alphabetically lists articles about people, places, doctrines, important words, customs, and geography of the Bible.

The New Bible Dictionary, edited by J. D. Douglas, F. F. Bruce, J. I. Packer, N. Hillyer, D. Guthrie, A. R. Millard, and D. J. Wiseman (Tyndale, 1982) is more comprehensive than most dictionaries. Its 1300 pages include quantities of information along with excellent maps, charts, diagrams, and an index for cross-referencing.

Unger's Bible Dictionary by Merrill F. Unger (Moody, 1979) is equally good and is available in an inexpensive paperback edition.

The Zondervan Pictorial Encyclopedia edited by Merrill C. Tenney (Zondervan, 1975, 1976) is excellent and exhaustive, and is being revised and updated. However, its five 1000-page volumes are a financial investment, so all but very serious students may prefer to use it at a library.

Unlike a Bible dictionary in the above sense, *Vine's Expository Dictionary of New Testament Words* by W. E. Vine (various publishers) alphabetically lists major words used in the King James Version and defines each New Testament Greek word that KJV translates with that English word. *Vine's* lists verse references where that Greek word appears, so that you can do your own cross-references and word studies without knowing any Greek.

Vine's is a good basic book for beginners, but it is much less complete than other Greek helps for English speakers. More serious students might prefer *The New International Dictionary of New Testament Theology*, edited by Colin Brown (Zondervan) or *The Theological Dictionary of the New Testament* by Gerhard Kittel and Gerhard Friedrich, abridged in one volume by Geoffrey W. Bromiley (Eerdmans).

A **Bible atlas** can be a great aid to understanding what is going on in a book of the Bible and how geography affected events. Here are a few good choices:

The Macmillan Atlas by Yohanan Aharoni and Michael Avi-Yonah (Macmillan, 1968, 1977) contains 264 maps, 89 photos, and 12 graphics. The many maps of individual events portray battles, movements of people, and changing boundaries in detail.

The New Bible Atlas by J. J. Bimson and J. P. Kane (Tyndale, 1985) has 73 maps, 34 photos, and 34 graphics. Its evangelical perspective, concise and helpful text, and excellent research make it a good choice, but its greatest strength is its outstanding graphics, such as cross-sections of the Dead Sea.

The Bible Mapbook by Simon Jenkins (Lion, 1984) is much shorter and less expensive than most other atlases, so it offers a good first taste of the usefulness of maps. It contains 91 simple maps, very little text, and 20 graphics. Some of the graphics are computer-generated and intriguing.

The Moody Atlas of Bible Lands by Barry J. Beitzel (Moody, 1984) is scholarly, very evangelical, and full of theological text, indexes, and references. This admirable reference work will be too deep and costly for some, but Beitzel shows vividly how God prepared the land of Israel perfectly for the acts of salvation He was going to accomplish in it.

A **handbook** of biblical customs can be useful. Some good ones are *Today's Handbook of Bible Times and Customs* by William L. Coleman (Bethany, 1984) and the less detailed *Daily Life in Bible Times* (Nelson, 1982).

For Small Group Leaders

The Small Group Leader's Handbook by Steve Barker et al. (InterVarsity, 1982). Written by an InterVarsity small group with college students primarily in mind. It includes information on group dynamics and how to lead in light of them, and many ideas for worship, building community, and outreach. It has a good chapter on doing inductive Bible study.

Getting Together: A Guide for Good Groups by Em Griffin (InterVarsity, 1982). Applies to all kinds of groups, not just Bible studies. From his own experience, Griffin draws deep insights into why people join groups; how people relate to each other; and principles of leadership, decision-making, and discussions. It is fun to read, but its 229 pages will take more time than the above book.

You Can Start a Bible Study Group by Gladys Hunt (Harold Shaw, 1984). Builds on Hunt's thirty years of experience leading groups. This book is wonderfully focused on God's enabling. It is both clear and applicable for Bible study groups of all kinds.

How to Lead Small Groups by Neal F. McBride (NavPress, 1990).
Covers leadership skills for all kinds of small group—Bible study, fellowship, task, and support groups. Filled with step-by-step guidance and practical exercises to help you grasp the critical aspects of small group leadership and dynamics.

The Small Group Letter, a special section in *Discipleship Journal* (NavPress).
Unique. Its four pages per issue, six issues per year are packed with practical ideas for small groups. It stays up to date because writers discuss what they are currently doing as small group members and leaders. To subscribe, write to Subscription Services, Post Office Box 54470, Boulder, Colorado 80323-4470.

Bible Study Methods

Braga, James. *How to Study the Bible* (Multnomah, 1982).
Clear chapters on a variety of approaches to Bible study: synthetic, geographical, cultural, historical, doctrinal, practical, and so on. Designed to help the ordinary person without seminary training to use these approaches.

Fee, Gordon, and Douglas Stuart. *How to Read the Bible For All Its Worth* (Zondervan, 1982).
After explaining in general what interpretation (exegesis) and application (hermeneutics) are, Fee and Stuart offer chapters on interpreting and applying the different kinds of writing in the Bible: Epistles, Gospels, Old Testament Law, Old Testament narrative, the Prophets, Psalms, Wisdom, and Revelation. Fee and Stuart also suggest good commentaries on each biblical book. They write as evangelical scholars who personally recognize Scripture as God's Word for their daily lives.

Jensen, Irving L. *Independent Bible Study* (Moody, 1963), and *Enjoy Your Bible* (Moody, 1962).
The former is a comprehensive introduction to the inductive Bible study method, especially the use of synthetic charts. The latter is a simpler introduction to the subject.

Wald, Oletta. *The Joy of Discovery in Bible Study* (Augsburg, 1975).
Wald focuses on issues such as how to observe all that is in a text, how to ask questions of a text, how to use grammar and passage structure to see the writer's point, and so on. Very helpful on these subjects.